Edward Hind

Songs of Mercia, in Two Parts

Comprising poems secular and spiritual

Edward Hind

Songs of Mercia, in Two Parts
Comprising poems secular and spiritual

ISBN/EAN: 9783337006686

Printed in Europe, USA, Canada, Australia, Japan

Cover: Foto ©Thomas Meinert / pixelio.de

More available books at **www.hansebooks.com**

SONGS

OF

MERCIA,

IN TWO PARTS;

COMPRISING

𝔓oems, 𝔖ecular & 𝔖piritual.

―――

BY EDWARD HIND.

―――

NOTTINGHAM:
PRINTED BY J. AND H. CLARKE, CLUMBER STREET.
1863.

PUBLISHED JANUARY, 1862, IN ONE VOL., 8mo.

HESPER :
Visions and Verses, or, from Hell to Heaven.
BY EDWARD HIND.

Though many of these poems have appeared, first of all, in the periodical press, they are all possessed of a solid worth, which distinguishes them from the trivial ephemera of the hour; and though they have a directly religious purpose, which is so frequently the death of poetry, they are genuine bursts of song, their devotional character never degenerating into the dismal and the dull. Some of the "Visions", such as those in which the poet beholds in wrapt ecstacy of soul the Mercy-seat and the Christ, are truly sublime in their conception, and as regards their form, are embodied in stately and harmonious numbers. Mr. Hind is never more happy, than in some of his contributions to the hymnology of his native land; of these we give a few specimens, taken almost at random, from the closing pages of the volume.—*Stirling Observer.*

Too often religious poetry, or rather what is dignified by that name, is the very worst of poetry, sometimes a mere wild rhapsodizing, sometimes a mere sickly sentimentalism done in verse, and that not always good verse. But Mr. Hind's poetry, though religious, is good. It is serious, without being sad—devout, without being dull. Far from the melancholy whine, which some seem to regard as an essential element in religion and religious writing, it is honest, manly, and vigorous, as well as pious. The first eighty pages of the book are devoted to a series of visions—visions of Grace, God, Life, Christ, Man, Time, Sin, Hell, Death, and This World and the Better Land. The remaining 120 pages contain a number of beautiful sonnets.—*Ayrshire Express.*

Taken as a whole this is unquestionably the best work Mr. Hind has as yet produced; and examining it in detail, we could easily point out passages which would do our poets of a national fame no discredit. The scenery of the visions is often a faithful reminder of the landscapes of dreamland, and some of the descriptive epithets are very finely chosen. In one or two instances, a daring of imagination is shown, which the general reader will not, perhaps, wish to advance one step further, but, in the main, considering among what subjects the author moves, his fancy shows due reticence. The latter portion of the work will most probably give the fullest satisfaction, since it appeals to more varied tastes. Some of these brief lyrics may hereafter be introduced in collections of hymns, with much advantage to worshippers.—*Nottingham Review.*

INDEX

TO FIRST PART OF SONGS OF MERCIA.

SECULAR POEMS.

Angel of Home	71
Angel of Time	17
Armour, Christian	88
Boy, Sonnet to	59
Bride's Chorus	28
Bridegroom's Chorus	28
Brook, Little	5
Canary	73
Castle, Nottingham	109
Castle, The Ruined	15
Children, Little	72
Childhood, Cowslips of	6
Childhood, Emigrant's Dream of the Home of	64
Childhood, Home of my	100
Child and Moon	90
Chorus, The Bride's	28
Chorus, The Bridegroom's	28
Chorus, Procession	29
Christian Armour	88
Church of his Fathers, Emigrant's Dream of	66
Church on the Hill	22
Civilization, Soul of	102
Conflict of Powers of Good and Ill	58
Cowslips of Childhood	6
Day, The Wedding	1
Double Trouble	99
Dreams, Vision of	60
Dew-drop and Sun	76

Emigrant's Dream of the Church of his Fathers	66
Emigrant's Dream of the Home of his Childhood	64
Epithalamium	11
Exiles, Songs of English	105
Fish, The Little	96
Free, Sea of the	63
Friend, On Marriage of	102
Garden, my Grandfather's	95
Good and Ill, The Conflict of	58
Hall's Marshall, Monument	88
Hill, Church on the	22
Home, Angel of	71
Home, Emigrant's Dream of	64
Home of my Childhood	100
Hope, Love's First	16
Jehovah in Judgment	78
Last Request	108
Life, Nature's Happy	2
Life, The River of	23
Life and Wife	13
Little Children	72
Little Fish	96
Lost Ones, Voices of	87
Love's First Hope	16
Love's Prescience	58
Lovers, Return of	26
Love, Sighs of	9
Love, Song of	10
Loving Ones, Voices of	86
Marriage of a Friend	102
Marshall Hall's Monument	88
May, Merry Month of	8
Memory, The Violets of	21
Moon, The	107
Moon and the Child	90
Mountains of Wales	94
My Grandfather's Garden	95

Nature's Happy Life	2
New Zealand to Old England	111
Nottingham Castle	109
Old England, New Zealand to	111
Palace of Temptation	31
Prescience, Love's	58
Pretty Canary	73
Procession Chorus	29
Request, The Last	108
Return, The Lover's	26
River of Life	23
Ruined Castle, The	15
Sea of the Free	63
Sighs of Love	9
Skylark, The	3
Song of English Exiles	105
Song of Love	10
Song of the Little Brook	5
Sonnet to a Boy	59
Soul of Civilization	102
Spring, Song of	61
Spring, Valley of	14
Sun and the Dewdrop	76
Sun's Vesper Song	24
Swallow, Sceptical	91
Temptation, Palace of	31
Time, Angel of	17
The Skylark	3
Trent, Vale of the	98
Trouble, Double	99
Vale of the Trent	98
Valley of Spring	14
Vesper Song, The Sun's	24
Violets of Memory	21
Vision of Dreams	60
Voices of Loving Ones	86
Wales, The Mountains of	94
Wedding Day, The	1
Wife and Life	13

INDEX

TO SECOND PART OF SONGS OF MERCIA.
SPIRITUAL POEMS.

Advent of Peace	73
Affliction	43
Angel of Death	31
Angel of Faith	8
Angel of Peace	16
Chaos, Man's	44
Childhood of Heaven	67
Confirmation, Psalm of	69
Death, Angel of	31
Despondency	33
Dirge, Rifleman's	84
Doubt	14
Dream, St. Peter's	36
E. K. H., In Remembrance of	58
Evil and Good	7
Exiled Gods	25
Experience, Psalm of	29
Faith, Angel of	8
Gods Exiled, The	25
Good and Evil	7
Heart, Keep Thy	35
Heaven, Childhood of	67
Heaven, Psalm of	60
Humanity, Psalm of	70
Hymn, Morning	52
Influence, The Invisible	24
Innocence, Psalm of	13
In Remembrance of E. K. H.	58
Judgment, Psalm of	55

Keep Thy Heart	35
Lament, Mother's	83
Life March of	42
Man's Chaos	44
Mansions of Rest	52
March of Life	42
Mercy, Psalm of	15
Morning Hymn	52
Mother's Lament	83
Ode	61
Orison	20
Patience	11
Peace, Advent of	73
Peace, Angel of	16
Peace, Psalm of	57
Praise	6
Psalm of Confirmation	69
Psalm of Experience	29
Psalm of Humanity	70
Psalm of Heaven	60
Psalm of Innocence	13
Psalm of Judgment	55
Psalm of Mercy	15
Psalm of Peace	57
Psalm of the Soul	46
Psalm of the Temple	5
Reason and Revelation	76
Rest Eternal, Mansions of	52
Rifleman's Dirge	84
Sabbath	4
St. Peter's Dream	36
Sincerity	81
Soul, Psalm of the	46
Supplication	19
Temple, Psalm of	5
Thanksgiving	79
The Good Lord Pardon Every One	54
Vice and Virtue	68
Word and Witness	77
Worship	72

POEMS.

THE WEDDING DAY.

Across a fair valley which spread far around
To the distant blue hills that encircled the scene;
I wandered one day, o'er the grass-covered ground,
That bloomed in the springtide's most beautiful sheen.

I roamed with delight under white-blossomed boughs
Of hedges that ran o'er the flower-covered sod,
Where the minstrels of nature were breathing the vows
Of the worship, whose music ascended to God!

When lo! to a broad-rolling river I came,
On whose bosom of silver the season's pure light
Was sparkling in showers of heavenly flame,
Whose beauty and brilliancy dazzled the sight.

And there on the bank of the stream, as I stood
Watching its waters roll on in their pride;
With white sails outspread o'er the crest of the flood,
A vessel swept down on the breast of the tide :

A numerous and gay bridal-party that bore,
Sailing slowly along like a cloud through the sky,
Who inviting me into their bark from the shore,
I stepped in at once as the vessel passed by.

And slowly we sailed down the waters so clear,
To the sound of sweet music, while floating along,
That arose from our boat through the sun-lighted air,
To which all the company chanted this song :—

NATURE'S HAPPY LIFE.

See nature's happy life awake,
And greenly bud o'er bush and tree,
Whose little feathered minstrels make
The groves resound with melody.

The streams are sparkling in the sun;
And with the influence of the time
Their waters now more brightly run,
And more melodious seem to chime.

Arrayed in sunshine, Spring descends
Along the incense-breathing air;
And lovingly o'er earth she bends
To bless the flow'rets blooming there.

As with the snow-white clouds she glides
Across the blue expanding skies,
O'er which her silver chariot rides,
Before whose steeds the winter flies.

As this strain's dying echoes rolled over the vale,
Two friends at my side began singing this song,
Which sweetly arose on the breath of the gale,
As by the green meadows we floated along :—

THE SKYLARK.

FIRST FRIEND.

List! to the lark that so sweetly is singing,
His song of delight in the region above,
As through the sunshine of nature he's springing,
Warbling his anthem of beauty and love;

BOTH TOGETHER.

Hail! to thee happy bird!
Ever with pleasure heard:
True is thy love-song, and tender thy strain;

Sweet as the voice of day,
Singing the song of May,
Showers thine harmony o'er the green plain.

SECOND FRIEND.

Higher and higher he's still mounting o'er us,
Sweeter and clearer his melody showers,
Warbling the beauty that's smiling before us,
Sparkling in sunbeams and blushing in flowers;

BOTH TOGETHER.

Hail! to thee happy bird!
Ever with pleasure heard:
True is thy love-song, and tender thy strain;
Sweet as the voice of day,
Singing the song of May,
Showers thine harmony o'er the green plain.

As this song o'er the valley rolled sweetly along,
We saw through the meadows a pretty brook glide,
And a lady on board began singing this song,
As we passed where the waters fell into the tide:—

SONG OF THE LITTLE BROOK.

I'm a quiet little brook, and I'm running all the day,
Through the pleasant sunny nook where the poet loves to stray,
Over pleasant fields of grass, whose trees their shadows throw
O'er my waters as they pass where the pretty daisies blow.

The morning's brightest glance upon my stream is shed,
As she strikes her golden lance into my silver bed,
Where the smooth dark pebbles rest, and the round white pebbles gleam,
Like jewels in the breast of my clear and crystal stream.

I'd rather be a brook than aught that I survey,
In my quiet grassy nook, where I'm singing all the day;
For I'm free from storm and strife as I glide my banks between,
And never in my life have a day of sorrow seen.

The stream to which I run, oft tells me of a sea,
Such greatness I would shun, for a brook I'd rather be;
For no tempest can alloy the music of my peace,
Or destroy the simple joy whose content can never cease.

Let me run among the fields, and rejoice among the flowers,
In obscurity that shields from every storm that lowers,
While the pretty birds to drink around my waters throng
And pause above my brink to repay me with a song.

As she finished, a meadow appeared to our sight,
With clusters of cowslips bespangled all o'er,
On which, as our company gazed with delight
I chanted this song by that flower-covered shore :—

THE COWSLIPS OF CHILDHOOD.

Behold! where the beautiful cowslips are blowing,
As they blossomed of yore in the days when we went
To gather the flowers that sweetly were growing,
In the green-sunny fields on the banks of the Trent,
'Twas there in a troop we ran shouting together,
As the golden young cowslips appeared on the green;
And with spirits reflecting the pure sunny weather,
In childhood we roamed o'er the beautiful scene.

Delighted we gazed on each field that around us
Appeared like a rich mine of treasures untold,
Whose precious attractions like avarice bound us,
As gleamed o'er the greensward its garlands of gold.

Like Cæsar the Rubicon passed—we together
The rivulet crossed that rose up to our knees,
And rejoicing went on through the clear sunny weather
To pluck the sweet cowslips that waved in the breeze.

Oh! green were the meadows and gay was the morning,
Fair flowers of the valley, on that happy day
Which shone on your clusters the landscape adorning,
And blessed the sweet flowers which bloomed on our way;
And light as the sunbeams of morning were dancing
On the beautiful breast of the clear-gushing Trent;
So fine were the joys on our soul that were glancing,
As o'er the green fields of the valley we went.

How clear is that far recollection of childhood,
As bright as the breast of this fresh-flowing stream,
Meandering away by the side of the wild-wood,
Reflecting it now like a beautiful dream.
Just so to our manhood, the valley elysian
Appears where in childhood we passed the swift hours;
Oh! it shines on our soul like a heavenly vision,
With its birds and its sunshine, its trees and its flowers!

As I ended my song, the musicians before us
Began playing a lively and soul-stirring strain,
To which all our company chanted this chorus,
As we sailed by a grove that arose o'er the plain :—

THE MERRY MONTH OF MAY.

The fields are growing fairer,
The woods are glowing green,
The streams are running clearer
That roll along the scene ;
The air is growing lighter,
The gardens blooming gay,
And heaven is smiling brighter,
In the merry month of May.

The birds their songs are singing,
From every budding tree,
As Spring o'er Britain's flinging,
Her smiles from sea to sea ;
Till all the isle is flowering,
With vernal life to day,—
The land in leaves embowering,
In the merry month of May.

As they sang, a white cottage arose o'er the flood,
With a garden behind and a grass-plot before,
Displayed on an eminence flanked by a wood,
Which stretched down for miles by the side of the shore.

And lo! in the garden, apparelled in white
A golden-haired maiden was gathering flowers,
Who smiled on our souls like an angel of light,
As slowly we sailed by her beautiful bowers.

And as her fair image arose o'er the plain,
A youth in the boat struck a love-breathing lyre,
To which in a sweet voice he chanted this strain
To music, that nature's self seemed to inspire.

SIGHS OF LOVE.

Blessings on that gentle breast,
Beauty's down, affection's pillow,
Where I long my head to rest
Like a bird upon the billow.
Oh! sweet love! my heart is sighing,
Thine to bless whate'er betide me,
While to heaven my prayers are flying,
That I soon may rest beside thee!

How! I long the gem to capture,
Rich as avarice e'er could span,
Trembling with the sweetest rapture
Woman ever gave to man!
Oh! sweet love! my heart is sighing,
Thine to bless whate'er betide me,
While to heaven my prayers are flying,
That my life may rest beside thee.

As he finished; behold on the opposite shore,
Another white cottage arose o'er the flood,
By whose porch of wild-flowers surrounding the door,
A jet-black haired maid in her innocence stood.

And as the sweet breeze bare us slowly along,
Another youth, touching his love-breathing lyre,
Breathed over the water this soul-witching song,
To music, affection's self seemed to inspire :—

SONG OF LOVE.

To look but upon thee is pleasure divine, love!
What where the rapture of making thee mine, love!
Oh! were I the lover, who soon shall embrace thee!
Oh! were I a king, in a palace to place thee!

Thy soul's like a dewdrop, all sparkling and bright, love !
Gemming a rose with its diamond of light, love !
Would I, like another, thy couch could fall on, love !
To melt in thine arms, and be mingled in one, love !

How sweet smiles thy soul on the sadness of mine, love !
Lighting my life with the gladness of thine, love !
And wakening the music now singing to me, love !
That yet I shall live to be wedded to thee, love !

So let the storm of my destiny roll, love !
There is peace in my heart, there is light in my soul, love !
And dead must my brain be, and pulseless my heart, love !
Ere that light is extinguished, that hope can depart, love !

As this song's tender echoes were dying away,
Our musicians a chorus breathed over the tide,
To which all the company chanted this lay
Of joy to the bridegroom and joy to the bride :—

EPITHALAMIUM.

Ever bright may the morning of love shine upon you !
And make you both happy as mortals can be,—

May the mercy of providence ever smile on you,
And many sweet summers of joy let you see!
May your home ever be by prosperity lighted,
And sorrow ne'er darken the light of your joy;
But your souls like a double star, heaven hath united,
E'er rejoice in the morn that no night can destroy.
Sweet o'er the union in which love has bound you,
E'er flow the sunshine of happiness round you,
Blessing the flowers with which love has crowned you,
And making your sweetest hopes ripen to joy!

Like an angel descending on this world of sadness,
Appears to our spirit the advent of love,
To give to this being a flower from the gladness
And beauty of that which is smiling above.
That angel has brought you this dearest of treasures,
Long round your hearts may her gift be entwined!
Blessing you both with the sweetest of pleasures,
Which amid all the thorns of this world we can find!
Fair as the heaven of joy smiling o'er you,
E'er may the future of life shine before you,
And as happy the memories that time shall restore you,
When your Spring to life's Winter its bloom has resigned!

As this chorus of happiness died o'er the wave,
A friend from the bridegroom requested a song,

Who immediately chanted this soul-stirring stave,
As our boat down the river moved slowly along.

LIFE AND WIFE.

How dreary the cot is, how weary the lot is,
Devoid of the charm which their care should beguile;
Though health may be found there, though wealth may abound there;
Yet wretched are both dear! without woman's smile.

But happy's the home, love! wherever we roam, love!
With a loving young angel its hearth to endear;
If man e'er can know, love! a heaven here below, love!
It only can flow from the smile of the fair.

Yes! blessed is the life, love! possessed of a wife, love!
To charm away strife, love! and sorrow's annoy:
So sweet is its pleasure, so great is its treasure,
That man cannot measure its rapture of joy!

As he finished this song, the musicians again
Began playing in concert a beautiful stave,
To which all the company chanted this strain,
As our bark glided on o'er the breast of the wave:—

THE VALLEY OF SPRING.

How lovely is the vernal scene,
Which spreads around us far away
In fields of tenderest, purest green,
And woods of grandly dark array;
Beneath the sparkling light of day,
The streams in floods of silver shine;
While hills afar their crests display,
And in one scene all charms combine.

What shall this happy valley sing,
Whose meadows now before us lie;
Just like the paradise of Spring,
Displayed beneath the cloudless sky.
Blessed scene of peace that wak'st the sigh
Of pleasure, as your fields we view;
How oft from future days shall fly
Remembrance back to gaze on you!

As this chorus went rolling afar down the vale,
A friend at my side began singing this song,
Whose music was borne on the breath of the gale,
As by a grey castle we floated along:—

THE RUINED CASTLE.

Behold where the hoary old battlements rise,
Of the castle afar on the crest of the steep:
That frowns like a storm on the verge of the skies,
As down through the heart of the country we sweep:
There the Normans once dwelt in the day of their pride,
When their chivalry ruled over England's domain:
And beheld down this valley, its bright river glide,
As they looked from their hills o'er the far-stretching plain.

And still the old castle appears on the scene,
Where its ramparts for ages have breasted the blast;
The monument grey of the days that have been,
That proclaims to the present the life of the past;
But where beauty once smiled, and where valour once stood,
Now nothing abideth but silent decay;
For just as we all are borne down on this flood,
Their life by time's stream has been carried away!

Sweetly this song o'er the green valley rolled,
Till its last dying echoes expired on the plain,
Like memory's last sigh o'er the lost—when behold,
A friend in our boat began singing this strain :—

LOVE'S FIRST HOPE.

Through fields of corn by yonder grove,
I wandered many a year ago;
My youthful bosom fraught with love
That sighed its future bride to know.

My fancy dwelt upon the thought,
And wondered who my bride would be:
And while for her my spirit sought,
I longed my future wife to see.

An empty void ached in my heart,
That what it knew not sighed to know,
And prayed affection to impart
What love alone can e'er bestow.

The gracious hope within me born,
How clearly I recall to day;
As through the growing fields of corn,
Alone I went upon my way.

That sweet hope like the guiding star,
The Magi's weary way beguiled,
Hath cheered my lonely life afar,
Till on my soul thy beauty smiled!

A friend from the bride next requested a song,
Who immediately charmed all our souls with this strain,
By a nobleman's seat as we glided along,
Which arose o'er the river that watered the plain :—

THE ANGEL OF TIME.

An angel of beauty abides on the earth,
Sent down to its orb from a region of bliss,
To smile on man's life at the hour of its birth,
And sing to our world of a happier than this ;
From which she first came to our cloud-covered shore
To breathe the sweet music which flows from her lyre,
In the language of angels that comes to restore
The speech of that heaven to which we aspire.

When the night of affliction envelopes the soul,
She sings of that land where no sorrow can be,
O'er whose vallies for ever the morning shall roll,
In whose glory our spirit no shadow shall see ;
When the flower of affection first springs in the breast,
Its beauty she sings in such anthems of joy,—
They flow o'er the soul like the strains of the blessed,
United by love that no death can destroy.

When the prayer of repentance ascends from the sod,
Through the tears of contrition that water its sighs,
As sweet as the still gentle utterance of God,
Through her harp breathes the pity and peace of the skies;
When the psalms of men's praises to heaven aspire,
Then echoing the strains to which angels adore,
The music of worship ascends from her lyre,
Whose deep tones vibrate through the soul evermore!

When men by the might of injustice oppressed
To the Judge of mankind for deliverance cry,
Her voice like His blessing falls over their breast,
As she wafteth the prayer of their souls to the sky;
O'er the mother embracing her infant, she sings
In harmonies sweet as her love for the child,
Whose helplessness so to the tenderness clings,
Of the being who first on its innocence smiled.

O'er the patriot who falls for his country she mourns
In such tones as awaken men's souls from their sleep,
As she sings o'er the grave that his ashes inurns
In strains, from oblivion his memory that keep;

O'er the martyr who dies in the cause of mankind,
Her strains like the chant of heaven's worship resound,
Transforming the fires on earth round him twined,
To the glories with which he in heaven shall be crowned.

As we stand by the grave where departed friends lie,
More sweet than the teardrops upon them which fall;
Around us, her heaven-breathing harmonies sigh
Of a love that transcends the affection of all;
Which the loved and the lost to our soul shall restore
In a region from which we shall look upon this
As angels look down on our thorn-covered shore
From their morning celestial of glory and bliss!

The beauties of nature she chants in such strains
As enrapture the nations around which they roll;
As she sings of the seas, rivers, mountains and plains,
And sun-throning heavens encircling the whole;
Not a throb of our bosom, or thought of our brains,
But she utters in song of such beauty and power,
As 'mid all that is mortal, immortal remains
Ever bright as a star, yet as sweet as a flower.

When the soul of the poet by wrong is oppressed,
She opens above him the gates of the skies,
And shows to his spirit the thrones of the blessed,
As they smile over death from their sorrowless skies;
Till his heart melts in tears to the music of love,
And he sighs out his prayers from this thorn-covered sod,
Confiding his cause to the justice above,
And attuning his harp to the mercy of God!

So Poetry wanders across the broad earth
Our sadness to soothe and our pleasures to cheer,
With the music of that world from which she came forth
Its blessing to breathe o'er this sorrowful sphere;
Attracting from wrong by the grandeur of right,
Transforming men's prayers into praise as they rise,
And casting o'er nature a love-beam of light,
To guide up man's soul to its home in the skies!

As she finished, we came to a wood-shaded green,
Where the scent of sweet violets arose on the air;
And as all enraptured we gazed on the scene,
An old man began singing this violet-song there:—

THE VIOLETS OF MEMORY.

How sweet was the time when in childhood I strayed
Beside the green bank where the violets were born,
Where I first saw the sweet flowers bloom in the shade,
And caught their perfume on the breath of the morn.
My father first guided my steps to the scene,
And showed me the nook where the violets were found,
All hidden like gems in their coverts so green,
Whose leaves overshadowed the moss-covered ground.

And there the sweet violets are blooming to day,
In the spot where my childhood first gazed on the flowers
Which faded so fast from my vision away,
With all their bright circle of swift-flying hours;
But, though violets again in their coverts may bloom,
No Spring to my life shall its childhood restore,
Or call back the father who sleeps in his tomb,
To take me to gather the violets of yore!

As this song sweetly sighed o'er the violet's green bower,
The valley spread out as our bark sailed along,
And afar on the blue hills appeared a grey tower,
To which a maid sang this appropriate song:—

THE CHURCH ON THE HILL.

Look upon yon hoary pile,
Standing on the rising ground,
Seen afar for many a mile,
With yon ancient fabric crowned;
History's landmark! fixed on high,
It hath stood six hundred years,
Placed betwixt the earth and sky,
Where its hoary tower appears.

Round it twenty ages sleep,
In their long and last repose,
Wrapped in slumber dark and deep,
Which on earth no waking knows;
They've all had their little day,
Ours on us is shining bright,
Ere it also pass away,
Let's be happy in its light!

As this song down the valley was dying away,
Our band began playing the same as before,
To which all our company chanted this lay,
As we sailed past a village that stood on the shore :—

THE RIVER OF LIFE.

Oh! could we all sail down the river of life,
As together we float down this beautiful stream,
To the sound of sweet harmony, far from all strife,
And lighted by nature's most life-stirring beam:
Ever seeing fresh beauties the further we went,
As new scenes we discover as onward we glide,
Whose attractions such charms to our journey have lent,
As down we have sailed on the river's broad tide.

How sweetly existence would then glide along:
No sorrow to trouble, no care to annoy;
Our life set to music just like a love-song,
Ever sighing its pleasure and singing its joy;
But, alas! such a lot were too happy for man,
So let's make the most of this short little day,
And enjoy all the happiness in it we can,
For see as we're singing 'tis passing away!

As they finished their song:—o'er the river's clear breast,
The sun's waning light in a rich flood was thrown,
As slowly he set in the far-distant west
O'er the wood-covered hills in his glory that shone;

And as over heaven he cast his last rays,
Illuming the earth with their beautiful beams,
We sang altogether this song in his blaze,
As slowly we sailed o'er the breast of the stream :—

THE SUN'S VESPER SONG.

We gazed on the sun's golden orb in the west,
As he smiled like a god as he sank to his rest,
While the clouds of the evening above him unrolled,
Like banners waved o'er him of crimson and gold ;
And sweet as its music o'er heaven is sung,
The sun's vesper anthem o'er nature was flung.

This morn when I burst through the shadows of night,
In my fire-winged chariot of glory and might,
The flowers unclosed in my life-blessing ray,
And birds began hymning the dawning of day,
As the kingdoms of nature awoke to the morn,
Whose beauty again out of darkness was born.

Upborne by my chariot of glory on high,
I sat like a god on the throne of the sky,
And smiled on my worlds, while I blessed with my beams
Your hills and your vallies, your woods and your streams,

Whose wide-spreading landscapes beneath me now lie,
As I look o'er your world with my heaven-piercing eye.

From the herbage which carpets the valley's low sod,
To the pine trees that girdle the mountains of God,—
From the vineyards that smile on the south's sunny plain,
To the fields of the north which its nations sustain;
Wherever the light of my presence could fall,
I have given my blessing to each and to all.

From the cottage embowered by trees in the dale,
To the castle whose battlements tower o'er the vale,—
From the hamlet which clusters around the grey spire,
To the city whose walls like a forest aspire:
As free as the breath of the life-blowing wind,
I have cheered with my presence the homes of mankind.

From the childhood at play on the quaint village green,
To the grey-headed grandsire watching the scene;
From the lovers betrothing themselves in my rays,
To the families chanting their eve-song of praise;
From the heights of the hills to the depths of the glen,
I have blessed with my light all the children of men.

And as on your being my blessing doth flow,
So men on each other your blessing bestow,
And mirror below as I image above,
The light and the life of the Father of love,
Whose goodness my great orb of glory designed,
To bless and to brighten the world of mankind!

As my daybeam to you doth his mercy convey,
So man to your brother His goodness display;
And your life shall like mine be by virtue made bright,
To reign o'er a heaven of love and delight;
And your death like the sunset now shines on the west,
A passage of peace to the land of the blest!

As the sound of this chorus was dying away,
Four friends in our bark began chanting this song,
Which sweetly arose o'er the close of the day,
And down the broad valley went rolling along :—

THE LOVERS' RETURN.

Lightly our boat o'er the waters has bounded,
As down the river we've joyously passed,

By the clear heaven of nature surrounded,
Whose last golden gleam on our haven is cast;
Onward we've sailed till the eve-star hangs o'er us,
Shining afar o'er the crest of the wood,
Fronting the height where our home smiles before us,
Casting a glow on the face of the flood.

Sweet as the teardrops of lovers when meeting,
After the absence that's parted for years;
When to each other their souls are repeating
Joy that can only be uttered by tears;
Over the water our strain is ascending,
To the dear friends by affection adored,
Whose welcome of love with our accents is blending,
As to our home they behold us restored!

As they finished, our vessel ran in to the land,
Where a stately white mansion its portals displayed,
And here as we stepped from the boat to the strand,
We beheld a procession before us arrayed.

With banners behind and with garlands before,
And music that sweetly arose o'er the tide,
As our party was drawn up in state on the shore,
Where twelve maidens in white sang this song to the bride:—

THE BRIDE'S CHORUS.

May life, dear lady! for thee twine
Its fairest flowers to bless thee,
May happiness be ever thine,
And sorrow ne'er distress thee;
But may thy life, dear lady, prove
A stream for ever springing
Beneath the light of happy love,
Sweet music ever singing.

Then turning to the bridegroom, next they sang
This song in honour of his nuptial day,
Whose melody across the water rang,
And down the country sweetly rolled away:—

THE BRIDEGROOM'S CHORUS.

We wish you on your wedding day
All good that time can bring you,
May fortune to your life convey
All blessings she can fling you;
May love unto your life impart
Affection's dearest treasures,
And happiness e'er bless your heart,
With never-fading pleasures!

Then with banners and garlands all waving around,
And music that blithely arose o'er the throng,
We marched on in pairs o'er the flower-covered ground,
With the people before us all chanting this song :—

PROCESSION CHORUS.

Joy on this auspicious day !
To the bridegroom and the bride,
Fortune shed her brightest ray,
On your happy fireside ;
May with good your life be crowned,
Pleasure wait upon your youth,
And with happiness be crowned,
The union of Love and Truth !

May your love but stronger grow,
As your years with time increase,
Never cloud a shadow throw,
To eclipse your smiling peace ;
Providence your life befriend,
Answering all affection's prayers,
Heaven ! its choicest blessings send
Over all your future years !

And so we passed on to the house from the shore,
To taste all the pleasures that fortune could give,
And enjoy such a feast as we ne'er had before,
In the home where I hope that delight may e'er live.

And there all our company stopped for the night,
As happily past as the beautiful day,
That so sweetly had flown on the wings of delight,
To the music of love, o'er the flowers of May. *

THE PALACE OF TEMPTATION.

Upon a dark and cloudy summer-night
Which had succeeded to a sultry day,
A minister was sitting by the light
That round his study cast its lonely ray;
Writing a sermon which he meant to preach
Upon the sabbath on the last command;
In which he sought his little flock to teach
How they might best temptation's power withstand.
No sound disturbed the stillness of the night,
For all within the house had sank to rest;
Excepting him, who had sat up to write
About the truth upon his soul impressed.
When suddenly a flash of lightning gleamed
Like an archangel's sword athwart the gloom,
And brightly on the good man's vision streamed
Through the uncurtained windows of the room;
And as the lightning seemed to pierce his eyes,
His ears were deafened by a startling peal
Of thunder that went roaring round the skies
Beneath whose crash the world appeared to reel;
While all the clouds from heaven seemed to fall
Upon the manse in stormy floods of rain,
Beating upon each roof and gable-wall
As water-spouts go dashing o'er the main.

Startled a moment from his usual calm,
The good man breathed to heaven a silent prayer,
And feeling then secure from every harm,
Resumed his usual calm demeanour there ;
But not without a feeling of surprise,
That not an inmate of the mansion seemed
Disturbed by all the uproar of the skies
Whose vivid lightnings round creation streamed.
As thus the good man thought the matter o'er,
Some person knocking at a furious rate,
Bade him at once unbar the bolted door,
To learn who it could be that knocked so late ;
Which, when he'd done he saw four horses stand
All harnessed to a covered carriage there,
Beside whose panting steeds with whip in hand
A questionable figure did appear :
In long black cloak and slouching hat arrayed,
Concealing both his features and his form,
Leaving alone a long red beard displayed,
Which like a meteor streamed amid the storm ;
And ere the worthy pastor could request
His business with him, or his name demand,
The stranger drew a letter from his breast
Which with a bow he placed within his hand :
On opening it this summons met his eye—
" Lord Arnon's compliments to Mr. Tait,

And begs that he immediately will try
To reach the castle ere it is too late;
Upon most urgent business that requires
His presence here before the night is gone;
And trusting he'll reach us ere two hours expire,—
Lord Arnon's carriage will convey him on."
The good man did not hesitate at all,
As this imperious missive met his eye,
For ever ready at his Master's call,
He always was prepared for duty's cry;
So stepping backward, through the lamp-lit hall,
His hat and best black coat he on him cast;
And folding round his chest a plaided shawl,
He through the doorway to the carriage pass'd;
And off was driven through that eerie night,
Whose blazing lightnings played around his form,
Shooting o'er heaven in streams of vivid light
Unto the ceaseless thunders of the storm.
He thus was whirled for many a mile away,
And what was strange, the road o'er which he sped
Appeared unknown to him, though many a day
He'd crossed the route that to the castle led.
Although he ne'er had gazed upon its walls,
The features of the district well he knew,
Which spread around its gay majestic halls,
Quite different to those that met his view;

Perplexed to account for this—he thought it might
Be caused by that wild tempest in the air,
Rushing on wings of fire along the night,
Making familiar objects strange appear.
And as he strove to find the old outlines,
The carriage turned abruptly to the right
Into a forest vast of gloomy pines,
Which like death's palace frowned upon his sight;
Making the minister at once suppose
The man who drove him must have lost his way,
Since no such forest as around him rose,
Could any district of his shire display.
But, yes! arising up on either hand,
As rapidly the carriage on was whirled,
Appeared the gloomy pine-trees' giant band,
Like genii frowning on a ruined world;
And as the vivid lightnings of the skies
With blinding brilliancy flashed through the gloom,
They seemed in dark and threatening forms to rise,
Guarding some awful realm beyond the tomb.
As the good pastor gazed in speechless awe
Upon phenomena so wild and strange,
As those whose eerie forms he darkly saw,
The scenery underwent a marvellous change:
The carriage passed into an open space,
Whereon no tree upraised its titan form,—

The thunder-clouds from heaven dissolved apace,
No traces leaving of the vanished storm.
And as to heaven the pastor raised his eyes,
Above his head the constellations shone,
With most surpassing lustre round the skies,
Bright as the hosts encircling Mercy's throne;
And suddenly above a distant hill,
The moon's full orb appeared before his sight,
Shedding o'er nature's bosom calm and still
The silvery beams of her serenest light.
With grateful feelings stirring in his soul,
The good man saw this welcome change prevail,
As down the carriage wheels began to roll
Along the green side of a lovely vale,
Which spread beneath him fair as Eden's lawn,
Erst smiled before our father Adam's eyes,
When first they were unclosed in nature's morn,
To gaze upon his sinless paradise.
Upon an eminence of this green vale,
That rose beyond a clear and crystal flood,
Whose silver stream meandered through the dale,
A glorious and majestic palace stood;
As vast in its proportions as the halls,
Where stood the throne of Babylonia's kings,
Yet graceful as a Grecian shrine, whose walls
Before the soul to perfect beauty springs;

It shone before the good man's wondering eyes
As white and dazzling as an alp of snow,
Above which spreads the grandeur of the skies,
And o'er whose front the fires of morning flow:
Built of the whitest marble, polished bright,
Its pillars—vast facade, and towering walls,
With garlands blazoned were of glorious light,
Like constellations shining round its halls,
Whose fires reflected on its dazzling frame,
Made it appear before the pastor's eyes
Just like a palace built of silver flame,
Resplendent as the gates of paradise.
Astonished, past all thought—the good man gazed
Upon this glorious and majestic sight
In speechless wonder, more than all amazed,
To think that he had ne'er before that night
Beheld or heard aught of the peerless halls,
Now bursting on him in a blaze of glory,
Just as Aladdin's magic palace-walls
Appeared before the Sultan in the story.
He had imagined, when the note he'd read,
His presence, that so pressingly desired,
That for some sick man on his dying bed,
His services that evening were required;
But now, he thought, while gazing on that fane,
That for some bridal feast or fête as gay,

For some cause which the event would soon explain,
He had from home that night been whirled away.
As the good minister was thinking so:
Across a noble bridge that spanned the flood
The carriage drove up to a portico,
Beneath whose pillars it arrested stood;
Upon whose steps the good man did alight,
And thence was ushered to a spacious hall,
By two tall footmen dressed in red and white,
Whose footsteps did before him noiseless fall.
From this first hall they to a second pass'd,
Whose grand proportions radiant with light,
As he a rapid glance around it cast,
Displayed a brilliant scene unto his sight;
Around a table which along it ran,
A youthful company were seated there,
Of lovely ladies and gay gentlemen,
Arrayed in dresses such as princes wear.
Rich piles of glittering gold and silver plate,
With every rare and delicate viand stored,
With more than all the pomp of regal state
Profusely covered that luxurious board,
While strains of sweetest music, through the hall,
Round which a thousand lustres cast their sheen
Seductively breathed o'er the festival,
And set to harmony the magic-scene.

If the good man had been at first amazed
With the exterior of that hall of light;
He felt much more astonished as he gazed
Upon the scene within that met his sight;
And ushered silently unto a chair,
Which vacant half-way down the table stood,
On that immense assembly seated there,
He gazed with eager eye and curious mood.
Their sole attention seemed entirely bent
Upon the luxuries that before them lay,
Talking and smiling as the rich wines lent
Their inspiration to that banquet gay;
Yet, as the good man eyed each brilliant guest,
He could not help but thinking something wild
And wicked on the assembly seemed impressed
That on his observation strangely smiled;
For he was living in the fairy days
When ghosts and witches haunted every clime,
Which now have all evanished in the rays
Of that intelligence that marks our time;
And as his eyes around the board did range,
He felt emotions of distrust and awe,
Whilst thinking of his introduction strange
To that unknown assembly which he saw;
For though the ladies all were young and fair,
And of a stately noble presence seemed

The gentlemen who seated with them were,
Sometimes he thought a strange expression gleamed
Across their features, fleeting as the fire
That flashes fiercely through the tempest's gloom,
And in the clouds as sudden doth expire,
Which for a moment its white forks illume.
Strange stories of the character and life
Of that young noble and his wicked crew—
Of profligate followers, with evil rife
Shot vividly his recollection through,
As he sat pale and silent at the board,
With such a mine of glittering treasures graced,
With such a heap of tempting viands stored,
Which he preferred, however, not to taste.
From this absorbed state he was roused at last,
By a tall gentleman of stately mien
Requesting to take wine with him as pass'd
The red decanters round the splendid scene;
But as he did so, o'er his features played
Such an expression of unearthly pain,
As made the pastor from him shrink dismayed,
And without utterance on his seat remain;
For as he gazed upon his neighbour's face,
He thought a shriek of agony must flow
Out of his writhing lips, on which the trace

Appeared of deep irremediable woe;
And as the pastor cast a furtive glance
Around the room on that assembly there,
Behold on every unknown countenance,
He saw the same unearthly look appear;
Which as he marked he felt a thrill of awe
Pass through his being like a deadly blast
Turning him white with terror as he saw
The awful look which o'er their features past.
Whilst all the fearful tales he'd ever read
Of devilry and witchcraft; through his mind
In one long sulphurous recollection sped,
As shoots a stream of lightning through the wind;
In this emergency his last resource
Was a small Bible which he always bore
About him as the pilot of his course,
Where'er he travelled upon sea or shore:
Resolved the first words he beheld should guide
His conduct there with wisdom from above,
Determined by its council to abide,
No matter what the consequence might prove;
All this had past much quicker than we can
Relate the story as it did transpire;
When opening his pocket-bible—the good man
Beheld these words before him flame like fire:—

" Look not thou upon the wine when it is red, when it giveth his colour in the cup, when it moveth itself aright. At the last it biteth like a serpent, and stingeth like an adder."

Refusing then the wine upon the plea
That he was pledged unto a fast that night,
Which must not on that evening broken be,
He felt his soul within him grow more bright;
As silent worship whispered in his heart,
Beseeching help from Jesu in that hour,
Entreating that He would to him impart
The strong defence of His protecting power.
When suddenly two doors were open cast,
Down at the bottom of that spacious hall,
Through which the numerous assembly passed
Between a corridor's white marble walls,
That to a vast conservatory led,
Containing fruits and flowers of every hue,
Which like a fairy-forest round it spread,
Blooming resplendently before the view.
The rarest plants of every far-off land,
The choicest flowers and fruits of every shore,
Displayed such beauties upon every hand,
As that good man had never seen before;

All placed beneath an artificial sky,
Which seemed of one vast sheet of crystal made,
And whose white star-shaped lamps were hung on high,
In systems round that lofty roof arrayed,
All grouped around a full-orbed silver moon,
Diffusing splendour through that aerial hall,
As fair as through the cloudless night of June,
The rays of Luna over nature fall.
The pastor marvelling such things could be,
Beheld the company around him move
Unto the sound of softest harmony,
Sweet as the tenderest sighs of happiest love;
Yet ever and anon across his breast,
Crept a dark feeling of distrust and awe,
Which on his mind at last the thought impressed
That 'twas the effect of sorcery that he saw;
As thus he mused with fascinated sight
Fixed on the gleaming fruits and glowing flowers,
That so profusely bloomed amid the light
That shone upon those paradisean bowers;
A lady, radiant with youth and grace,
Approached the pastor whose white hand did bear
A nectarine just plucked within that place,
Which with a smile she proffered to him there.
Referring to the book of books once more,
With marked mistrust that he could not control,

The following words appeared his eyes before,
And steeled against the syren's smiles his soul :—

"Let not thine heart decline to her ways, go not astray in her paths. For she hath cast down many wounded: yea, many strong men have been slain by her. Her house is the way to hell, going down to the chambers of death."

Declining, then, her offering, with a bow,
He from the lady blandly turned away
And left her scowling with an angry brow,
As if she meant such courtesy to repay:
But, he kept moving with the crowd along
To that conservatory's utmost bound,
And so at last was carried by the throng
Into a spacious garden's vernal ground,
Which seemed to spread for miles on every hand,
As the good man with wonder and delight
Beheld its noble trees before him stand,
Where that surpassing garden met his sight:
Bright with rich parterres of the gayest flowers,
A lovely scene indeed it was to see,
As choirs of singing-birds in its green bowers
Warbled the strains of nature's harmony,

Hailing the first unclouded golden gleam
Of morning breaking through the eastern skies,
Lighting the garden with resplendent beam,
As over it the sun began to rise,
And fountains round it, too, began to play,
Shooting their waters to a dizzy height,
And falling back again in showers of spray,
In marble basins of the purest white,
Where swarms of gold and silver fishes played,
Themselves disporting in the waters clear ;
As gleaming whitely from each distant glade,
The statues of the gods shone through the air.
Broad avenues that led to grass-plots green,
Dotted with trees, beneath whose vernal shade
Ladies and gentlemen were resting seen,
On every side to him their charms displayed,
While lovely lakes beyond them he descried,
Which bright as silver in the sun did glow,
Whereon fair troops of snow-white swans did ride
In graceful motion gliding to and fro.
On the good pastor ever slowly went,
With feelings strange of fear, distrust and awe,
Surpassed alone, by his astonishment,
At those fair scenes which he around him saw ;
When lo ! another lady, fairer still,
Than was the first who had so sweetly smiled

Upon him when she sought to move his will,
Yet who with all her charms had not beguiled,
Approached him with a bouquet in her hand,
Composed of roses red and roses white,
And with a smile that he could scarce withstand,
She proffered him her present of delight,
Which for a moment his resolve did shake—
Not to touch anything within that place,
Making him half extend his arm to take
What was presented with such winning grace,
When "touch not, taste not, handle not," he read,
As glancing at his oracle, he withdrew
His arm again and from her turned and sped
As fast as he could walk the garden through:
When suddenly he saw before him there,
A massive temple of black marble shine,
Heavily looming through the morning air,
Built for what purpose he could not divine;
Passing a doorway that did open stand,
Strange was the sight his vision then embraced—
Two rows of black bronze vases on each hand,
Upon pedestals of red granite placed,
Those filled with gold coin on the right hand wall,
Those on the left hand, full of silver coin,
Both rows of vases stretching down the hall,
Till at its bottom they appeared to join;

These heaps immense of treasure thus disposed,
The climax formed of all that he had seen,
As he looked on their masses quite afraid,
Wondering from whence such wealth had gathered been.
As thus he mused, a gentleman in black
Accosted him with gay and courtly smile,
Bidding him, if he felt of wealth a lack,
To haste and seize upon its glittering spoil :
"Since all who enter in this hall," said he,
" Are welcome to whate'er they like to take
This lucky morning, by the last decree,
This treasure's master but last night did make."
At first the good man strongly felt disposed
To take a portion of that wealth away,
As temptingly itself to him disclosed,
As to a hunter does his lawful prey ;
" For with a handful of this wealth," thought he,
" I can relieve the poor for many a day,
Transform to happiness their misery,
And charm for ever all their cares away."
Before he acted on this thought, howe'er,
He thought he'd at his Bible look again,
Whose oracle thus spake unto him there,
Before he'd any of that treasure ta'en :—

"Your riches are corrupted, your gold and silver are cankered. Blessed is the man that endureth temptation: for when he is tried, he shall receive the crown of life, which the Lord hath promised to them that love him."

Declining then to act upon the advice
Of that smooth gentleman arrayed in black,
The plausible stranger vanished in a trice,
As on him there the pastor turned his back.
And on the good man passed beyond recall,
Through a small doorway in that room he found,
Which opened out into another hall,
Whose bright black marble walls were hung around
With countless rows of polished silver keys,
Hanging on golden nails the walls all o'er,
Thick as spring-blossoms flower on apple trees,
In rows that reached the roof and touched the floor:
And in the centre of this hall, behold,
There sat a most benevolent-looking sage,
Whose snow-white beard unto his girdle rolled,
Proclaiming thus his venerable age,
Who as the minister approached him, rose,
And bowing to him with serenest grace,
Exclaimed—"I was beginning to suppose
No pilgrim e'er again would reach this place,

But I am glad to see there yet is one
Who can the palace of temptation pass,
And all the blandishments and dangers shun,
Which have destroyed so many souls, alas!
But by what spell have you the power defied,
Of all the enchantments of yon house of fear,
Which could they but have drawn your steps aside,
I never should, my son! have seen you here?"

The pastor drawing forth his Bible said,
While placing it within the stranger's hand,—
"Behold the councillor that has hither led
In safety through yon dark and dangerous band."

" Aye!" said the venerable-looking sage,
" You could not fail with such a heavenly friend,
To walk aright upon your pilgrimage,
By it conducted to a happy end."

" But," said the pastor, " what becomes of those
Who passing through temptation's dangerous throng
Reject the only guide that can disclose
The right way to them—and must needs go wrong?"

"After, in sin, their season has been passed,"
The venerable sage to him replied,
"Into a sleep by opiates they are cast
Unto them given as they God's grace deride,
And in their slumber, demons come who bear
Them bound in chains unto death's sunless shore,
Where they at last awaken in despair,
To find themselves its captives evermore."

Shuddering o'er what this answer did disclose,
The pastor said, "pray, sir, can you declare
What is the meaning of these countless rows
Of silver keys which hang around us here?"

To whom the stranger thus replied, "my son!
To every pilgrim who has safely passed
The palace of temptation as you've done,
A silver key is given here at last,
That will unlock for him the golden door
Of that bright city which exists above,
Whose palaces arise upon the shore
Of perfect beauty and perpetual love."

"But, how shall I attain this city fair?"
The pastor said,
     To whom rejoined the sage—

" By passing through yon little doorway there,
You can at once commence your pilgrimage ;
For issuing thence—a green and spreading plain
Spotted with golden flowers will meet your eyes,
O'er which you'll pass till you its boundary gain,
Beyond which you'll perceive a forest rise,
Through which you will proceed along a glade,
O'er which at last you'll see a mountain rise,
Whose base is buried in the forest's shade,
And whose proud summit's lost amid the skies,
Up this great mountain you must then ascend,
Until its topmost steeps you can behold,
When bright above your pathway will impend
The shining city's battlements of gold ;
Whence on your ears the heavenly strains will roll,
Whose music will almost make you expire,
With ecstacy—as breathes upon your soul,
The chanting of the blessed celestial choir :
The grace invoking of the Holy One,
You must advance unto the gates of gold,
That shining on you glorious as the sun,
Your dazzled vision will afar behold,
Whose lock you'll open with the silver key,
Which I will give you, when you will perceive,
What ne'er before your mortal eye could see,
Nor ever yet your earthly heart conceive."

"Give me the key! Oh venerable sire,"
Exclaimed the good man, "and let me depart:
With what a longing do your words inspire
The faith that long has worshipped in my heart!"

Smiling, the old man gave the silver key,
With a small wallet, holding food beside
Which lay beside him, "go in peace," said he,
"The road you walk on safely there will guide.'

"Farewell!" the pastor answered as he took
With thanks the little wallet and the key,
"I hope upon the city soon to look,
And soon within its walls to welcome thee."

"Farewell!" replied the venerable sage,
"I do not think it will be long before
I shall be summond on my pilgrimage,
By the Great King unto its happy shore."

So saying, the little door he open cast,
And on his pilgrimage the pastor sped,
To find the country over which he passed,
Exactly as the good old sire had said;

He quickly crossed the green and golden plain,
Traversed the forest, reached the mountain's base,
And soon the dizzy heights he did attain,
Whence he beheld afar the heavenly place,
Whose golden battlements, and glittering walls,
And gates of glory shining like the sun,
As far surpassed temptation's earthly halls,
As o'er man's life ascends the Holy One.
As towards those glorious walls the good man pressed,
Such heavenly strains of music breathed around,
Rolling from that bright city of the blessed,
As turned him faint and breathless with the sound:
The grace invoking them of earth's Great King,
He nearer drew unto the city's walls,
Above which he beheld sublimely spring
Ten thousand temples and majestic halls,
Which far above his head did grandly tower,
As o'er night's plain the alps of morning shine,
Wearing the impress of eternal power,
And crowned with glory by a hand divine;
Whence smiling on him in immortal youth,
Fair as the day-star shines from morning's skies,
Robed in the brightness of eternal truth,
Angelic forms appeared before his eyes.
With speechless wonder ecstacy and awe,
The good man stood beneath the city-walls

And thrust the key into the door, he saw,
When from those glorious shrines and glittering halls,
Such strains of music vocal made the wind
With such transporting bursts of rapture there,
That he awoke and suddenly to find,
That he was sitting in his old arm chair.
And by the golden beams of morning's light,
Which did around his study brightly stream,
He saw that all the startling scenes of night
Were but the airy phantasms of a dream;
Exhausted with his unrelaxing toil,
And all the writing which he had to do,
As he sate studying by the midnight oil,
Suddenly nature claimed of him her due;
And as beneath her power he sank to rest,,
From something mightier still had flashed the beam,
That had revealed the city of the blessed,
And photographed the pictures of his dream.
That marvellous dream the minister related
Unto his flock upon the sabbath-day,
And on its moral thus expatiated,
Instead of preaching what he meant to say.

"My youthful hearers! do you not perceive
This dream which perhaps was sent me for your sake,

Contains a moral you may well believe,
And act upon when you are wide awake.
You must like me pass through temptation's halls,
Which will before you all their charms display,
To ensnare your youthful souls within their walls,
And turn your footsteps from the better way;
By one means only can your life withstand,
The allurements sin will spread before your eyes,
By taking on the Word of God your stand,
Whose Spirit only, man can render wise,—
Thus and thus only can your souls endure
The trials that will come to test you all,—
By this and this alone can you secure
The victory, where so many thousands fall;
For like twin-angels walking at your side,
God's Word, and spirit of your prayers shall go,
And through the snares of ill shall safely guide
Your souls to good, too bright for earth to know;
But should you these two councillors despise,
And from their heavenly wisdom turn away,
Oh, never then upon your darkened eyes
Shall dawn the glories of eternal day;
But down the precipice of cureless woe
Your souls for ever will be headlong cast,
When you, but oh! too late! will wake to know
The truth that from you for a lie you cast.

You poorest boys are rich in priceless wealth,
Since you possess a reasonable mind,
You're rich in youth and hope, and strength and health,
And soul immortal in your being shrined ;
Oh ! act not like the prodigals who cast
The priceless treasures of their life away,
And, then too late, discover at the last
That they are given to evil as its prey ;
But, oh ! be wise, my youthful friends, in time,
And so employ the wealth by you possessed,
That it may purchase in a deathless clime
A bright inheritance amongst the blessed.
We often see announced upon the walls,
The short-lived pleasures that so soon are o'er,
Like clouds that borne through nature's aerial halls
Upon the winds return to us no more.
The only entertainment that is worth
A man's deliberate choice and constant care
From this world stretches past the life of earth
Unto the morning of a brighter sphere :
This entertainment which surpasses all
The light vain pleasures that aught else can give,
Is what a true philosophy would call,
The life that but a christian soul to live ;
For there's no entertainment that can prove
So entertaining as a virtuous life

In harmony with heavenly truth and love ;
And but with earthly hate and ill at strife.
And since Religion's power alone can give
This greatest entertainment to the soul,
I would enforce its power on all who live,
That it might guide them to its heavenly goal.
Some people at Religion sneer in sooth,
But, oh! Religion is as high as heaven,
And nothing on the earth can lower its truth,
Or from it take the power that God has given :
Resplendent as the sun above our head,
There's nothing that can make its glory fade,
As solid as the world on which we tread,
Naught can convert its substance to a shade.
No men or nations ever mourned at last
The acts they let Religion's power control ;
But many have to ruin down be cast,
Because they'd flung its glory from their soul.
For on the mind Religion sheds a ray.
Which draws it upward towards the source of right,
Where men without its guidance go astray,
And down for ever sink in error's night,
And deep in ill as we see myriads fall,
As high in good their spirit now would soar,
If but their wasted life they could recall
To choose the guide they did reject before.

Then, little children! let Religion guide
Your steps through all the dangers of your way,
For there is nothing you can choose beside,
Can lead your life to God's eternal day;
It only can the happiest hopes of youth
Convert to flowers of ever-blooming joy,
And bless your being with the immortal truth,
That e'en the stroke of death cannot destroy.
It only can the power and patience give
All ill to vanquish and all wrong to bear,
And make you through life's sufferings rightly live,
Until the reason for them shall appear.
Then, to Religion let your heart be given,
And when the life is o'er, that nature gave
It, like God's angel shall descend from heaven,
To guide you through the darkness of the grave;
When from your lips as trembles earth's last breath,
And on your spirit lightens heaven's first beam,
You will discover through the night of death,
The truth whose glory will surpass my dream!"

THE CONFLICT OF THE POWERS OF GOOD AND ILL.

The conflict of the powers of good and ill,
Shakes the great globe with their opposing odds;
Making the bosom of the bravest thrill,
To see the giants battling with the gods;
Viewing the thunderbolts of vengeance hurled
In streams of lightning through the affrighted skies,
Waking the great artillery of the world,
Whose volley to the thunder's roar replies,
Death! to whatever power mad man defies!
When past his rage shall rise a nobler state
Than that of which we hear the expiring cries
Amid the wars that nations desolate,
For over all this strife, yet peace shall bloom,
And liberty shall stand on slavery's tomb.

LOVE'S PRESCIENCE.

Dear love! I never can believe,
My hope to win thy heart a dream;
For like the golden star of eve,
Arising o'er yon silver stream:
That hope upon my soul doth gleam,
Like heaven's bright answer to the sighs,

Have oft invoked that blissful beam
Of sweet affection from the skies!

Oh no! my love cannot despair,
Though thou wert lost and I were dead,
'Twould rise immortal from my bier,
Sweet love! past death, and thence would shed
Unending blessings on thy head,
Pure as the prayers I've breathed for thee,
Which from the heaven to which they've sped,
Have said thou shalt their answer be!

SONNET TO E. S. H., A BOY A YEAR OLD.

Thy rill of life has just began to run,
Oh may it to a glorious river flow,
Illumined by the light of Wisdom's sun,
May it rejoicing down time's valley go,
While fragrant zephyrs o'er its bosom blow,
Dimpling its current into sunny smiles,
On which may never storm a shadow throw,
To dim the heaven-born grace, whose beam beguiles
God's innocent streams with blessing naught defiles,
As they rejoice beneath love's golden reign,
And on expanding run round thornless isles
Of heaven-born happiness unto the main,
In which thy stream of life must end at last
To rise to heaven, I pray, when earth is past!

A VISION OF DREAMS.

Upon my couch at midnight I reclined,
    Whose star-lit heavens evanished from my view,
As unto slumber I myself resigned,
    When lo! this vision dawned before my view.

I dream'd I saw before my being rise
    The cot beneath whose roof my life was born,
Round which, methought, were spread the cloudless skies,
    Irradiant with the glory of the morn.

As thus my childhood's home smiled o'er the scene,
    I round it saw again the white doves flying,
And watched the wee pet lamb frisk o'er the green,
    On which the old dog "Dash," again was lying.

And as I gazed I saw my sire once more,
    Smoking his pipe beneath the chesnut tree,
And then I saw my mother at the door,
    Smiling again as once she smiled on me.

Whilst all the memories of my childhood's home
    And recollections of departed hours,
Methought like life's first flowers did round me bloom,
    And covered with their garlands childhood's bowers.

And as my being stood enchanted there,
  Before my eyes appeared a white-robed child,
Just like a fairy-angel, wondrous fair,
  Who on me like my little sister smiled.

Then clasping mine within her little hand,
  Said come with me beside yon brook to stray,
To pluck the pretty flowers along the strand,
  And gather garlands on the meads so gay.

So there, methought, we did together roam,
  Reclining sometimes on the pretty flowers,
And often looking back upon the home,
  Which smiled upon us from its vernal bowers.

When as we there reposed on nature's breast,
  The sound of music rose amid the trees,
And childrens' voices near our place of rest
  Thus breathed this happy song upon the breeze :—

SONG OF SPRING.

What softness through the air is sighing,
  What music floats upon the gale,
As Spring, with her green banners flying,
  Comes proudly marching down the vale.

What flowers beneath her feet are springing,
  What bloom within her smile is born,
What birds around her path are singing,
  Whose beauty brightens nature's morn.

What love from her sweet life is glancing,
  What light from her bright presence flies,
Which over earth with morn goes dancing,
  And casts her glory on the skies.

What beams of joy from her are gushing,
  What garlands blooming on her trees,
What beauty from her life is blushing,
  Whose fragrance floats upon the breeze.

What softness through the air is sighing,
  What music floats around the dale,
As Spring, with her gay banners flying,
  Comes proudly marching down the vale.

Lo! as that song went echoing down the plain,
  One side of heaven, methought, did roll away,
Disclosing to our view the purple main,
  Which far beneath the earth's horizon lay.

Across whose breast, methought, white sails did shine
    As to and fro they glided o'er the deep,
When from a bark that sailed upon the brine,
    This song, methought, upon our ears did sweep :—

THE SEA OF THE FREE.

Hast thou gazed on the breast of the sun-lighted sea,
Which spreads its blue waves round the land of the free,
Where the far-flashing billows rush on to the roar
Of the foam-crested surge as it breaks on the shore;
As the day-beam of heaven descends o'er the sea,
Which rolls its blue waves round the shore of the free?

O'er its billows the great ships of free commerce shine
Which spread their white wings o'er the breast of the brine
As in fleets they depart to some far-distant shore
And return to the "Isle," whence they journeyed before,
While the daybeam of heaven descends on the sea,
Which spreads its blue waves round the shore of the free.

And oh! it is glorious again to behold
The wide-spreading waters around us unrolled,
That stretch far-away to the verge of the sky,
Till lost in the distance that melts from the eye

While the daybeam of heaven descends on the sea,
Which rolls its blue waves round the shore of the free.

Lo! as this song came rolling on us there,
  And o'er the landscape sweetly died away,
A sound of distant music filled the air,
  And o'er the sea a voice did chant this lay:—

THE EMIGRANT'S DREAM OF THE HOME OF HIS CHILDHOOD.

I dream'd that I sate in the home of my childhood,
With my brother again at my dear mother's knee,
And together we gazed on the green-spreading wildwood,
That o'er the bright river first shone upon me;
Again in his arm-chair my father sate smiling
Within the old room I remembered so well,
Which fronted the valley whose meadows beguiling,
Appeared round the home, where we once used to dwell.

Again through the casement the maybeam was shining,
By which the laburnums displayed their bright flowers,
With lilachs and snowballs together combining,
In the gay little garden that used to be ours;

And by the old pictures my vision was greeted,
As my father's and mother's dear voices did chime
In the songs of my childhood, as they were repeated
Again as we sate in the long-vanished time.

And as o'er the meadows our chorus was ringing,
My sister came in, in the pink frock arrayed
With the blue sash around it, and joined in the singing
Like light o'er the water that pleasantly played,
And friends glided in, once so kind and true-hearted,
To repeat all the words which they uttered of old,
Ere laughing together, they rose and departed,
Where no more in this world I their forms shall behold.

I awoke from my dream and my tears began falling,
O'er the vision of home I shall enter no more,
I awoke from my dream and my soul began calling,
To the Father of man who alone can restore;
In brightness unfading and beauty undying,
The home, friends, and childhood, earth could not retain,
For the soul that beyond all its sorrow and sighing
Shall behold them, and bless them, and clasp them again!

Lo! as this strain sighed o'er the vernal bower,
  I saw afar the ancient church arise,

And dark against the sky display the tower,
   Which in the past once stood before mine eyes.

And as I gazed upon the hoary shrine
   Across the ocean sighed this sweeter strain,
Just like an exile's breathed across the brine,
   Unto the land he ne'er shall see again :—

THE AUSTRALIAN EMIGRANT'S DREAM OF THE CHURCH OF HIS FATHERS.

I dreamed that afar in the church of my sires,
   I worshipp'd again as I worshipp'd of old,
And repeated each prayer which God's Spirit inspires,
   Beseeching His grace on the sheep of His fold;
Once more the old roof of the church shone upon me,
   Supported by pillars the same as before,
Again through the windows I saw smiling on me,
   The Sabbath of childhood that smiled there of yore.

Once more my dear mother beside me was kneeling,
   As the voice of the minister rose on our ears:
Again we stood up while the organ was pealing
   And sang the sweet psalm of the long-vanished years.

Once more from the pew where so oft we were seated
I beheld the old faces beneath me restored,
As again by the singers the hymn was repeated,
Which the Father of all for his mercies adored.

Once more on my bosom the influence was glowing,
   That sweet as God's blessing on man's spirit falls,
Again through my soul was the breathless speech flowing
   Which the pilgrim of earth to the Mercy-Seat calls,
And once more like the first golden beam of the morning,
   The smile of God's mercy descended on me,
Connecting the darkness of time with the dawning
   Of the glory of that world hereafter to be.

I awoke from my slumber and sweet thoughts were fling-
   Their happy emotions of joy o'er my breast,   [ing
Like the church bells of yore o'er the green churchyard
   ringing,
Where the sabbath of England so sweetly did rest,
And I knelt to the throne of the Father beseeching,
   For the faith and the feelings of childhood again,
And for grace I besought just to pity the teaching,
   Which the world gives to man in its desert of pain.

Lo! as that song was rolling down the plains,
　　We rose and wandered o'er the thornless flowers,
Hoping that we might hear more happy strains,
　　Setting to music childhood's passing hours.

Until methought we came unto a brook,
　　Through which I rushed unto the other side,
Where, as for my companion I did look,
　　A lovely maiden did before me glide.

Whose face, methought, blushed sweeter than the rose,
　　Whose eyes were azure as the heavenly blue,
Whose arms gleamed fairer than the lily glows,
　　Whose aspect all surpassed I e'er did view,

Her robes of white were gemmed with stars of gold,
　　And floated round a form of matchless grace,
Round which a stream of golden ringlets roll'd,
　　And twined their tresses round her angel-face.

And in seraphic accents, whose sweet sound
　　Breathed on me like a maiden's sigh of love,
She said, now you have pass'd o'er life's first bound
　　And must with me across the valley move.

For childhood's cherub you have left behind,
  Whom naught on earth shall to your life restore,
Though you will oft look back and sigh to find
  The angel gone whom you shall see no more.

Wide is the valley which before us lies,
  Across whose fields your steps with me must go,
While Hope discloses to your youthful eyes
  The heaven-lit heights that she alone can show.

Look o'er the plain and tell me what you see,—
  I gazed where bursting through its fleecy shroud,
Methought a far-off landscape dawned on me,
  Appearing through a mass of breaking cloud.

And shining far-away across the plain,
  A chain of mountains did o'er nature rise,
Whose base was buried in the distant main,
  And whose eternal summits propped the skies.

And lo! upon the loftiest mountain-height,
  A crystal temple did before us blaze,
Whose glorious doors of ever-flashing light
  Shone like the gates of morn upon my gaze,

And on a lower steep than that, behold
    Another temple did before us shine,
Whose burning gates of brightly burnished gold
    Disclosed the entrance to a glorious shrine.

And far below the mountains' dizzy height,
    Upon a hillock at their feet, which rose,
A pretty cottage dawned upon our sight,
    With roses covered white as winter-snows.

Lo! said the angel, bursting on thy gaze,
    The far-off temple there of Fame doth shine,
And there the golden gates of Plutus blaze,
    Through which men enter into fortune's shrine.

While far below, arising like a cot,
    The happy home of sweet affection see,
Now look at all, young heart! and choose thy lot,
    For one, by time, will yet be given to thee.

Then I will choose affection's home, said I,
    Let others fame or fortune seek to prove,
But for the good of nature I shall cry,
    A heart to love me and a heart to love.

Lo! as I spake there fell of light a flood,
   Upon a plot of grass that cot before,
And there a man and woman smiling stood,
   With little children playing round the door.

Awakening in my soul the fond desire
   To go and rest upon that happy green,
When lo! that man, he struck a silver lyre,
   And warbled forth this song across the scene:—

THE ANGEL OF HOME.

You may sing as you like of the angels of bliss,
But give me an angel on earth I can kiss;
For wherever the fancy for angels may roam,
The dearest to man is the angel of home!
That angel who comes from the Eden above,
Arrayed in its beauty—inspired with its love,
With its light in her eyes, and its youth in her charms,
And grace in her form, and heaven in her arms,
To ennoble man's nature and hallow his life,
With that angel of beauty, a virtuous wife.
The angel of happiness, Mercy hath given,
To bless man on earth as she leads him to heaven.

Oh! dreary indeed would life's wilderness be,
Bright angel! bereft of affection and thee,
Who crown'st with love's flowers man's wild desert-shore,
And giv'st him the being he sighs to adore,
Who comes as his bride to his bosom forlorn,
To give him the pleasures that round thee are born,
And yield to his longing thy soft-glowing breast,
As a pillow of peace where his nature can rest.
And bestow the deep joy thou alone can'st impart,
By the kiss of thy love! to the life of his heart.
Bright angel of happiness! Mercy has given,
To bless man on earth as thou lead'st him to heaven.

And as this joyful song came rolling o'er,
   The landscape till afar it died away,
His silver harp the man did smite once more,
   To which the woman's voice and his did chant this lay:—

LITTLE CHILDREN.

Like the life of spring returning
   To the sultry summer's bowers;
When for their first life is yearning,
   All their drooping leaves and flowers:

Little children home come smiling,
   With the little words they bring;
And the pretty ways beguiling,
   Which our summer link with spring.

Home they bring the priceless treasures,
   Of their little innocent love;
Home they come like heavenly pleasures,
   Whispering of the joys above.
Here they rise like fountains springing,
   Over nature's desert-sod;
Fraught with music ever singing,
   Songs of happiness to God.

And as they ended too this happy strain,
   Which o'er the valley sweetly rolled along;
That man did strike his silver harp again,
   To which the children sang this pretty song:—

PRETTY CANARY.

Pretty canary! gay little fairy!
Art thou not weary sometimes of the cage?
Where thou art daily warbling so gaily,
As though thou loved really thy small hermitage.

Through our souls thrilling pipes thy light trilling,
All the house filling with carollings sweet;
Forwards now springing, back again singing,
Round the walls ringing, thy strains that repeat.

When we are peeping at thee while sleeping,
Thy little head keeping so close to thy breast,
Do'st thou in dreaming, e'er catch a gleaming
Bird, from the bright beaming Isles of the Blest. *

Through olive bowers, o'er myrtle flowers,
Fly the swift hours of joy in their clime,
Whose happy morning thy brothers are born in,
The prison all scorning that cages thy prime.

Oh! no such vision, bird! in derision
Brings their elysian gardens to thee;
Thy happy slumbers no grief encumbers,
Caught from the numbers that gush from the free.

So little urchin on thy pole perching,
As though thou wert searching for something to keep,
Gaily before us, bird! warble o'er us,
Sweet as the chorus they chant o'er the deep.

---

* *The Canary Islands.*

Pretty canary! bright little fairy!
Thy song is not dreary like doubt's bitter spring,
In silence now stopping as asleep thou art dropping
Thy pretty head popping safe under thy wing.

Lo! as this strain upon my ears did sound,
   From that fair scene of peace and love and light,
Methought the mountains sank into the ground,
   And all the landscape faded from my sight.

And all the grass beneath me changed to sand,
   And all the flowers before me turned to thorn,
And round me stretched a blasted desert-land,
   Through which alone I wandered on forlorn.

Beneath a sky which grew as dark as death,
   With tempest-clouds from which red lightnings played,
Whose pealing thunders took away my breath,
   As on I struggled more and more dismayed.

My bare feet bleeding wheresoe'er I trod,
   And hailstones beating on my naked form;
Till in despair I wept aloud to God,
   And cried to Him to save me from the storm.

When from the heavens sweet music seemed to sound,
    And, lo! afar I saw Hope's form of light,
Who o'er the clouds smiled from the far profound,
    As thence she breathed this song along the night :—

THE SUN AND THE DEWDROP.

A dewdrop at midnight it wept on a thorn.
On which in the darkness its being was born,
In silence it mourned in the desolate gloom,
To find itself shut in that storm-covered tomb,
Unlit by a star and uncheered by a ray,
To charm for a moment its darkness away.

When, lo! on its breast fell a goldbeam of light,
As the great sun arose in his glory and might,
And smiled on the soul of the dewdrop forlorn,
Till it shone like a star on the point of the thorn,
As in accents of glory he bade it arise,
From the night of the earth to the morn of the skies.

And the dewdrop arose with the lark from the sod,
And rejoicing went up in the smile of its God.

On the wings of the zephyrs that bore it away,
From the darkness of night to the glory of day,
Which obeying the mandate its monarch had given,
The dewdrop enthroned on the iris of heaven.

Lo! as I listened to this heavenly strain,
   Whose melody came rolling down the skies,
More doleful round me grew the desert-plain,
   And as I raised from earth my tear-fraught eyes.

Behold! the heavens above me changed to fire,
   Whose burning dome lit up the waste around,
O'er which a shape of darkness did aspire,
   That like the king of terrors on me frowned.

And as I gazed in fear that chilled my breath,
   A mighty earthquake shook the desert-strand,
And ghastly shining in their robes of death,
   Above their open graves the dead did stand.

And whilst the stormy thunders shook the skies,
   And subterranean thunders rent the world,
Lo! from the dead this chorus did arise,
   Whose awful utterance round the waste was hurl'd:—

JEHOVAH IN JUDGMENT.

Jehovah we saw in His chariot of fire,
As He rode on the death-darting clouds of the storm,
While the great mountains trembled o'er earth that aspire
As they shrunk from the darkness that mantled His form;
Right onwards He rode on His tempest-clouds wheeling,
With the fires of His vengeance around them upcurled,
While deep-rolling thunders before Him went pealing,
To far-blazing lightnings that flashed round the world.

We saw Him ride onwards with life-smitten wonder,
With all His fire-banners of lightning displayed,
With His storms riding on to the roar of their thunder,
And His angels around Him in battle arrayed;
And so He passed on with His clouds closing round Him,
Eclipsing the grave with their world-darkening gloom,
Whence shot the red bolts from the lightnings that
  crowned Him,
As He rode over earth like the fire-storm of doom.

As from the ghastly dead these strains did pour,
 Methought that vision faded from my sight,
And on I wandered as I went before,
 Along the thorny desert's doleful night.

When lo ! a fiery dart did smite my brow,
    And then another struck my naked breast,
And then a wizard cried :—" Come, yield thee now
    A captive to thy master thou had'st best."

And then, methought, he rushed upon me there,
    And struck me down and bound my helpless form
With chains of fire, to waft me to his lair,
    To which he bore me through the shrieking storm.

With many a cruel buffet, gibe and jest,
    Which mocked me for the hurts that he had given,
That seemed to scorch my brain and burn my breast,
    As if by mortal wounds my life was riven.

And so, methought, he bare me to a cave,
    On which no sun, or moon, or star e'er shone,
As dark as death and dismal as the grave,
    And there he left me with my wounds alone.

And thus, methought, for many a hopeless year,
    I groaned a captive in that sunless cave,
Abiding in it with the dread despair,
    That dwelt with me within that living grave.

Until at last my mind delirious grew,
   So long imprisoned in that silent cell,
Until asleep I saw and waking too,
   Around me swarm a host of fiends from hell.

Who cried, " Come down with us, down, down, and down
   Unto a dungeon dolefuller than this,
O'er which a darker night than death's doth frown,
   Around the horrors of a worse abyss."

And then, methought, they seized my shuddering frame,
   And bare me down on such a fearful way,
On which such awful shapes around me came,
   As if to seize upon their helpless prey.

I lost all consciousness, and when at last
   That long-despairing swoon of dread was o'er,
And reason darkly through my spirit passed,
   I found myself within the cave once more.

Still bound in chains a hopeless captive there,
   No sun, or moon, or star to shed a ray,
Upon the darkness of the long despair,
   In which a helpless captive still I lay.

And there, methought, again the sorcerer came,
    And mocked me for the sufferings I had borne;
And with his wand of fire did scourge my frame,
    And stabbed me with his scymetar of scorn.

Until he left me wasted, worn, and wan,
    While round my brain once more delirium played,
For pain my reason cast beneath its ban,
    That blindly at the last through madness prayed.

And in my great despair, I breathed to heaven,
    Methought such prayers as ne'er were breathed before,
And such an answer to my prayers was given,
    As ne'er before was sent from Mercy's shore.

For there, as reason prayed within its tomb,
    Three forks of lightning seemed to blind mine eyes,
Followed by thunder-peals which rent the gloom,
    And like God's presence seemed to shake the skies.

And brighter than the lightnings of the storm,
    Whose infinite flashes down through space were hurled,
Behold, there stooped from heaven an angel's form,
    Riding upon the thunders of the world.

White lightning seemed to shine around his form,
   Upon his brow there gleamed a crown of light,
And brighter than the flashes of the storm,
   The sword he carried of celestial might.

And as his form descended in my cave,
   It grew more glorious than the heaven you see,
As there, he said, " I come from Christ to save,"
   Touched with his sword my chains, and left me free.

Then said, " arise! and in the strength of prayer,
   Follow me, brother! to affection's bower,
Where o'er the tomb of all thy slow despair,
   To heaven-born happiness thy life shall flower.

He guided me unto an airy height,
   Where earth, and sea, and skies beneath us lay;
Resplendent with the noontide of the light
   Whose morning lit my childhood's happy way.

And there the chain of mountains rose once more,
   On which the fanes of fame and fortune smiled,
And there the cot with roses covered o'er,
   Whose songs of love had so my thought beguiled.

And as I hung enraptured o'er the scene,
    Choose, said the angel which thy track shall be :
For two paths now appear upon the green,
    Which shall be thine, depends alone on thee.

Can'st thou the wizard's hellish wrongs forgive,
    Whose sorceries blasted all thy tender youth,
Or wilt thou not for righteous vengeance live,
    And blast his soul with thunder-bolts of truth ?

Oh ! tempt me not, fair angel, then I sighed,
    What good to man by vengeance e'er was given ?
Oh, let whatever wrongs his life betide,
    Let him forgive who prays to be forgiven.

Then follow me, the angel smiling said,
    And I will lead thee to the heights above,
Where waiteth for thee now a virtuous maid,
    Conducted thither by the angel Love.

With eager step I hurried up the height,
    And there a lovely maiden on me smiled,
More fair than Hope once shone upon my sight,
    And innocent as boyhood's angel-child.

Her presence breathed the freshness of the morn,
   Her young life spread around my life like Spring,
Her virtue dewed with peace my heart forlorn,
   Her love brought to me all that heaven could bring.

Oh! sighed I, from the dungeon of the past,
   Faith brings my life at last, sweet maid, to thine,
As through the shadows round thy pathway cast,
   The angel Love, has brought thy life to mine.

And sweeter than the showers unto the sod,
   Dearer than all the treasures of this life,
Sweet! as the mercy of affection's God,
   Thou com'st to me, my love! my blessed! my wife!

And as I clasped her to my longing breast,
   The angels Faith and Love, our union crowned,
With that affection which makes nature blest,
   As o'er us rose sweet music's solemn sound.

And as we turned to learn whence came those strains,
   The heavens expanded over which they sung,
And like the mountains rose above the plains,
   Above their chain a monarch-mountain sprung.

On which a temple shore more white than snow,
    Whose glorious towers and majestic dome
Reared over earth its heaven-encircled brow,
    Sublimer than the earth-built shrine of Rome.

Above whose crest the heavens to ope appeared,
    Shedding a flood of gold upon the shrine,
That over earth its heaven-lit dome upreared,
    The future altar of a faith divine.

And lo! upon the dome as on a throne,
    Methought St. Paul appeared arrayed in white,
Who like a God, methought, on myriads shone,
    Who suddenly stood with us on our height.

He held a mighty scroll within his hand,
    Emblazoned with a golden Lamb and Dove,
Beneath which was inscribed this great command,
    In golden letters of the God of love.

"Your heavenly Father knoweth that ye have need of all these things, but seek ye FIRST the kingdom of God, and His Righteousness; and all these things
    SHALL BE ADDED UNTO YOU."

And whilst we gazed with wonder-stricken eyes,
  The temple's starry doors were open flung,
Through which, methought, sweet voices o'er the skies,
  Thus answered all the questions thus we sung.

Voices of Loving ones from Earth.

Shall we not meet again beyond the tomb,
  And in a brighter world than man's survey?
The faded flowers that once on earth did bloom,
  Arising fadeless in a happier day?

Voices of Lost ones from Heaven.

Yes! we shall meet again beyond the grave,
  And past the strife and storms of nature see,
The innocence that God to man once gave,
  Arising bright as immortality.

Voices of Loving ones from Earth.

Shall we not meet again, our lesson taught
  By all the many failures of the past?
And find the good that here we vainly sought,
  Abiding in its heaven-lit home at last?

Voices of Lost ones from Heaven.

Yes! we shall meet again beyond the ill,
   Whose power so often turned our steps aside,
And find the angel-good we sighed for still,
   Enthroned o'er death; the soul's immortal bride!

Voices of Loving ones from Earth.

Shall we not meet again beyond the hate,
   That marred so often here our peace and joy?
And taste the blessing of a sinless state,
   No strife shall trouble, and no storm annoy?

Voices of Lost ones from Heaven.

Yes! we shall meet again to speak the love
   To which but broken speech on earth was given.
And in God's paradise the affection prove,
   Whose prayers on earth have swelled the praise of heaven.

* * *

As over earth these anthems rolled away,
   I woke to find a dream had thus beguiled,
And there my wife and little children lay,
   Who on me in their slumber sweetly smiled. †

---

† NOTE.—This Vision of Dreams was first published under another title, June, 1862.

MARSHALL HALL'S MONUMENT,

(*Nottingham General Cemetery.*)

" A wise Physician, skilled our wounds to heal,
Is more than armies to the public weal."—HOMER.

Here rest the ashes of a good, great man,
Beneath a stone as solid as his fame,
Whose deep-discerning soul grasped in its span
The spinal truth of man's most wondrous frame,
And placed beside great Hervey's deathless name
The name inscribed upon this granite tomb,
Whose glory through the years of time shall flame,
The past records of science to illume,
And light her future march along the gloom
With clear effulgence and immortal ray,
Till truths as great are drawn from nature's womb,
As those which he discover'd in his day :
Whose dust beneath this monument is shrined,
Which aptly symbols his colossal mind !

CHRISTIAN ARMOUR.

When evil's darts our life assail,
   And wrong would fain our peace destroy,
What arms against them shall prevail,
   And keep secure our inward joy?

The arms, by which they're best withstood,
  Will be the choice of wisdom's will,
Whose power will turn to spurs of good,
  The darts designed as goads to ill.

And by the might of good alone,
  Whose life past evil's death doth live,
The shield can round our soul be thrown,
  Which can no injury take or give.

No hatred shall disturb our peace,
  And poison all our springs of joy,
But something better shall increase
  The good, that evil would destroy.

And for those arms my life shall seek,
  Which only to the right belong,
The arms which give unto the weak,
  The power that overcomes the strong.

Thus armed, amid destruction's fires,
  My peace shall stand above their flame,
Whose truth beyond earth's hell aspires,
  More strong than all its wrongful shame.

THE CHILD AND THE MOON.

A little child walking one eve with his sire,
Beheld the full moon o'er the landscape aspire,
Whose meadows beneath it all tranquilly lay,
Perfumed with the scent of the newly-mown hay.
O! father, look yonder, the infant did cry,
What a great, big, red orange is hung in the sky!
I never did see such an orange before,
And where it does come from, I don't know, I'm sure.
Please, father, may'nt I just run forward and see,
If I can't get that orange for you and for me,
How mother will stare with surprise and delight,
When yon orange we take to our cottage to-night.
Thus saying that little boy ran a great way,
As fast as he could, o'er the meadows so gay,
But when a long way had his little legs ran,
The orange seem'd further, than when he began
So he flung himself down on a haycock quite tired,
While afar gleamed the orange he so much desired,
And exclaim'd, as he gazed on its surface so bright,
I shan't take you home to our cupboard to-night.
And there on the grass, as exhausted he lay,
His father approached him and to him did say,
A much greater distance, my boy, you must run,
Before you arrive, at yon orange, my son.

For that orange is now running faster than you
Have ever done yet, or are likely to do,
For that orange a world is, which God has placed there,
And none but His hand may approach to its sphere.
Yet many are they like my son, who aspire,
To drag to their level somebody that's higher,
Which for something they mistake, much less than
And dream, they can easily put on their shelf, (themself
When, alack! to its life they can never come near,
So far above their's is its high-hearted sphere,
That as well might they grasp at the moon, like my boy
As attempt to extinguish the life of its joy.

THE SCEPTICAL SWALLOW.

A troop of young swallows, when summer was past,
From the land of their birth, began starting at last;
For something spake strongly to every one,
And bade them at once o'er the ocean begone;
And so one fine day o'er the billows they flew,
Till the land of their birth was departing from view;
When a sceptical swallow just paused on his track,
And said to his comrades, "I think I'll go back.

"For see! we are just losing sight of the shore,
And no other arises our vision before;

So I think I'll return to the land I can see,
For a land that I can't is no country for me!
You say there's a voice that now sings in your breast,
Of a far-away region of glory and rest;
Let that voice guide you forward, but pray excuse me,
If I'd rather be guided by what I can see.

" When we've wandered away from our own native land,
Are you quite sure you'll all reach your far-away strand?
I see but before you a desert of waves,
In whose bosom belike you will all find your graves;
You are seeking a shore that you never did see,
Which perhaps ne'er existed—betwixt you and me;
Your fancy has led to this very wild act,
But excuse me, who'd rather be guided by fact!

" Must we cast the experience of life to the wind,
To let a mere notion rule over our mind;
When, alack! if we once bid good bye to the shore,
I'm afraid we shall never see land any more!
You say some old birds who before us have past,
Have said we shall come to some haven at last;
But how can the witness by sense be believed,
Which belies the experience ourselves have received?

"A faith without knowledge may pilot your flight,
But as for myself, I shall trust but in sight ;
You are free to take faith as your compass, I trow,
And I am as free but to take what I know."
So saying the swallow flew back o'er the sea,
As fast as the wings of a swallow could flee,
And the shore he regained in the darkness of night,
Very weary and hungry, and wet with his flight.

But the morrow soon smiled all his hardships away,
As light and as warm as a bright summer-day ;
And circling around in the land of the free,
The swallow was blest as a swallow could be ;
But alas ! the frosts came, and the insects all died ;
And in vain through the air did the poor swallow glide ;
No food could he find on the keen-cutting blast,
And he perished of hunger and cold at the last.

But ere he expired there dawned on his sight,
A glimpse of a far-away region of light,
Which spread its green havens of peace o'er the main,
And welcomed his brothers to summer again ;
And there in its circle of ever-bright hours,
He beheld them all flying through evergreen bowers,

Where summer was shedding her glory and light,
As he was expiring in winter and night!

And so there's a something in man's soul, I wis,
Which speaks to his mind of a world beyond this,
To which science is blind, and that sense cannot see,
But which something yet higher demonstrates must be ;
And what is that voice to our being that's given,
But Nature's voice echoing the utterance of heaven ;
And if we can't trust it, what is there beside,
In life or in death we can trust as our guide ? ‡

THE MOUNTAINS OF WALES

How calm grew the billows and soft blew the gales,
    As swiftly we steered by the mountains of Wales ;
That grandly arose o'er the surge of the tide,
    Exalting to heaven the crests of their pride ;
As music the echoes awoke of their vales,
    As swiftly we moved by the mountains of Wales.

Oh! ne'er can the vast forms from memory be hurl'd,
    That arose like the titan-built towers of a world,

---

‡ First published in " *Nottingham Review*," September 5th, 1862.

In the light of the morning sublimely displayed,
   In grandeur enrobed, and in glory arrayed;
While music the echoes awoke of their vales,
   As swiftly we passed by the mountains of Wales.

Great ramparts of nature! that sweep from the shore,
   Of the sea, whence ye spring to the sky where you soar
When shall we again o'er the billows be borne,
   Where ye rest in the shadows and lights of the morn
While music the echoes shall wake of your vales,
   As swiftly we steer by the mountains of Wales.

MY GRANDFATHER'S GARDEN.

Many years ago now where the alms-houses stand,
   In the heart of the city, fair gardens once smiled,
Whose pleasant trees shaded the face of the land,
   From which I have often pluck'd fruit when a child;
For a garden, my grandfather, had in that spot,
   And my first recollections are linked with the scene
Whose pleasures can ne'er be by memory forgot,
   Which delights to look back on the days that have been.

I remember how quiet that spot used to be,
    As the noise of the city came murmuring round,
And like distant music kept playing to me,
    As silent I stood on the flower-scented ground;
And I well recollect with what childish delight,
    I beheld the round snowballs all sparkling with dew,
By the quaint summer-house which arose on the sight,
    Beneath the white blossoms beside it that grew.

What changes since then have come over my soul,
    What changes since then have swept over the scene!
Where the songs of the days of the past ne'er shall roll,
    Their music again through the bowers that have been!
Yet their echoes are lingering in memory still,
    And the flowers in my grandfather's garden that smiled,
In the breast of the man now awaken the thrill,
    Of joy, which they gave to the heart of the child!

THE LITTLE FISH.

A little fish, one summer-tide, lay basking in its beam,
As he floated down the current of a clear and crystal stream;
And as he on its surface lay, so pleasant and so bright,
He thus began to muse aloud while basking in the light.

See life upon the water smiles, as happy and as gay,
As is the clear unclouded light of summer's lovely day,
But death upon the picture falls so pleasant and so bright
As gruesome and as icy-cold as winter's eerie night.

And swim wherever I may swim, and do whate'er I like,
Why then the prey I shall become of some great greedy pike;
And do whatever I don't like, and glide where'er I can,
Why then the prey I shall become of some more hungry man.

Who perhaps when I am starving, will tempt me with his bait,
Which if it do not kill outright, so sad will make my state;
That in my agony absorbed, all sense I shall forget,
And rush quite blindly unawares into his wicked net.

To be a little fish like me, oh! pray how would man like,
The helpless victim to become of a fisherman or pike?
Oh! if I could but be a man, and man could be a fish,
I think that I should quickly change the state of nature's dish.

So spake that small fish to himself, while sinking to the
    stones,
Of the stream where he'd been basking; to save both
    skin and bones;
Who if he'd been a little man had wagged his little head,
But being but a little fish, he wagged his tail instead.

When an angler walking by the water overheard his
    thought,
And said poor little dainty fish, you don't wish to be
    caught,
Very natural for a fish, indeed, yet, if you were a man,
To catch whatever fish you could I fear would be your
    plan.

And so with more philosophers that we around may view,
Who deem quite wrong for No. 1, what's right for No. 2,
And do whatever, fish! we may right principles to act on,
What serves 'em right at No. 2, don't suit at No. 1.

THE VALE OF THE TRENT.

The sweet star of love o'er the valley is shining,
    As here I am roaming o'er Trent's grassy plain;

With the branches of summer above me entwining,
    And the bright river flowing beneath me again :
While I gaze on the green meadows stretching before me,
    And calm-flowing river that waters the scene ;
Till their peace like a spell of enchantment comes o'er me,
    As I wander alone o'er the valley so green.

Thou sweet star of love ! o'er the waters now gleaming
    From thy sphere in the gold-clouded skies of the West,
Ever smile on the valley o'er which thou art beaming,
    Like a spirit of light from the shores of the blest :
For thou lightest the scene with a sense of devotion,
    Through whose happy fields I am roaming again ;
And wak'st in my bosom a tender emotion,
    My wild-breathing harp strives to echo in vain.

DOUBLE TROUBLE.

The troubles that upon us fall,
    As trouble often will,
How apt some people are to call
    The punishment of ill ;
But when on them falls something sad,
    How quick they change their mood,

And call not judgments on the bad,
   But crosses on the good.

Together but these judgments place,
   How great the difference shown!
Our judgment in our neighbour's case,
   Our judgment in our own!
Oh! when shall we the wisdom know,
   And charity attain,
That would not double trouble's blow,
   But halve misfortune's pain!

THE HOME OF MY CHILDHOOD.

I think of the time in the far-distant past,
When I sate with my mother one sweet sabbath day,
Whose light we both knew, was the light of the last,
From our once happy home that our eyes should survey.
When fondly we gazed on the objects around,
As we sate in the home where so happy we'd been,
Where we felt that our life's recollections were bound,
As we sighed our last lingering farewell to the scene.

We departed next day from the home of my youth,
And never returned to its shelter again,

Yet brought from it all the dear memories of truth
And love, whose sweet life in my heart yet remain;
And oft on the evening remembrance did dwell,
Whose sunset unto us no time should restore,
Which smiled on us both as we sighed our farewell
To the hearth of the home where we sate nevermore!

From our home of prosperity sadly we past
Through the wilds of adversity, pilgrims to roam,
Whence oft through the clouds of misfortune we cast
A glance of regret on our heart-cherished home!
That home, o'er whose downfall my spirit desired
To build for the parents I loved, up again,
But my hopes on the tomb of my mother expired,
And the fortune once hoped for, I've yet to attain.

Yet under a roof of my own I recall,
The home to their children my parents once gave,
And think of them both till my tears o'er them fall,
As together they rest in the night of the grave;
Till I pray Him who man's best affections bestowed,
To unite us again on a happier shore,
And impart to the souls, through whose life it once flowed,
The love that from home shall be exiled no more!

ON THE MARRIAGE OF A FRIEND

Joy round the home of your heart, ever hover!
  Happiness smile on your marriage to-day!
Affection unite the fair bride and her lover
  In the happiest of unions that earth can display!
Joyous as music from bridal bells ringing,
Far over nature their harmonies flinging,
Arousing the echoos whose chorus is singing,
The marriage of hearts for whose welfare we pray!

Hail! happy pair! heaven's blessings attend you,
  Crown you with pleasure and keep you from pain,
And sweet little cherubs of innocence send you,
  In whose life both of yours shall be imaged again:
Fair as the love that your souls is uniting,
True as the vows which together ye're plighting,
Pure as the joy that your hearts is delighting,
With the blessing for which they have sighed not in vain.

THE SOUL OF CIVILIZATION.

When the forest can repudiate the soil on which it grows,
Civilization can repudiate the faith by which it rose;

The inspiring spirit of that faith is the God who formed
  mankind.
No higher inspiration could exalt the human mind.

'Tis this the aspiring spirit gave to soar on pinions free,
Whose daring flight has passed all bounds but God's
  infinity.

It has raised man above the past and o'er it raises still,
As high as God's exalted heaven o'er Jove's Olympian
  hill.

As o'er the idols of the past our living faith doth tower,
Above the wisdom of the past our knowledge too must
  flower.

The creed that petrified the past by mythology was
  given,
The faith of our progression thrones the God of earth and
  heaven.

'Tis this which gives its growth and greatness to the
  modern mind,
And shapes its laws and thoughts and deeds to comprehend mankind.

'Tis this which makes the modern dive more deep than
   ancient lore,
And his achievements far surpass what man has done
   before.

'Tis this which makes his genius still aspire along the
   unknown,
Upon the eternity of God, the mind of man to throne.

'Tis this which o'er the pagan past exalteth reason's wing,
And bids it higher ever higher towards its fountain spring.

The soul which has the wisdom of the modern world
   inspired,
Which the dull and little mind of man with god-like
   thought has fired.

Is not the dead mythology that by the past was graven,
But is the living faith which thrones the God of earth
   and heaven.

And thus our knowledge cannot fail, but like its spring
   must flow
In streams unending which no bounds of space or time
   can know.

Some may be frozen o'er by doubt that yet again shall run,
Expanding wider in the beams of wisdom's fadeless sun;

Whose glory naught shall e'er eclipse or ever take away,
But which around the world shall shed God's universal day.

Through all the storms of darkness now, whose gloom is round us cast,
As glorious as the face of God, this faith shall smile at last.

When the flowers can repudiate the sun by which they blew,
When the body can repudiate the soul by which it grew,

Our greatness can repudiate the faith by which it rose,
Our wisdom can repudiate the life by which it grows.

And if they ever from their form their living soul could cast,
Their body then would ossify as fossilized the past.

SONG OF ENGLISH EXILES IN AUSTRALIA.

Great land of our fathers! how often to thee
Our souls breathe a sigh from the ends of the earth:

How oft in our dream-haunted slumbers we see
Thy green-spreading vallies, dear land of our birth!
Where once in our light-hearted boyhood we trod
The meadows and woods of thy far-distant shore,
And watched blooming round us, the flowers of the sod
No spring shall again to our being restore!
Yes! often the scenes where in childhood we strayed,
In the watches of night does remembrance regain:
And oft by the streams where affection first prayed,
Over hearts cold in death does its music complain;
And around the wide world, over ocean's white foam,
The tear-uttered worship of memory is sighed,
To the land of our fathers, and love-hallowed home,
That never again on our vision shall glide.
The corn-covered hills that around us once lay,
The cloud-covered skies o'er their breast that arose,
The mists of the morning dissolving away,
The dew-spangled pastures and woods to disclose;
Oh! never again shall our vision behold,
As vernal they shone in time's long-vanished sphere,
Displayed in the light of the morning's pure gold,
With larks singing sweetly its harmonies there!
Yet often, dear England! though lost to our sight,
In spirit we'll roam o'er thy vallies and hills,
Where the morning now walks in the glory of light,
And the white dew of heaven its blessing distills;

We'll visit the spot where our farewell was sighed,
And roam by the stream where in boyhood we went,
And around the grey tower of Wilford we'll glide,
Arising afar on the banks of the Trent !
Great land of our fathers ! across the blue breast
Of the broad-spreading main which divides us from thee,
Like the dove that returned to the ark of its rest,
Our spirit reverts to the " Isle of the free !"
Ever green be thy fields ! ever blest be the bowers !
Where, shielded by heaven, thy daughters recline,
And ever by freedom exalted thy powers,
Till the white cliffs of England shall sink in the brine !*

THE MOON.

Planet of beauty, affection and light,
Rising o'er earth like the soul of the night,
Where the memory shines of the earth-hidden sun,
When the brief day of his glory is run ;
Bearing the smile of his love on thy brow,
Hail ! Queen of heaven, how lovely art thou !
When thy young crescent o'er nature is seen,
Smiling so calmly o'er heaven's serene,
Hung like an island of glory on high,
Set like a crown on the crest of the sky ;

---

* First published in "*Nottingham Review*," March 14th, 1862.

Bearing its infinite peace on thy brow,
Hail! Queen of heaven, how lovely art thou!
Over what ages hast thou cast thy light?
Gliding away on thy thought-passing flight
Riding along through the infinite blue,
On this sabbath-evening to shine on my view,
Breathing the music of praise from thy brow,
Hail! Queen of heaven, how lovely art thou!
Bright as a jewel, yet grand as a world,
Thou smil'st from the clear skies around thee outfurled,
O'er the seas and the shores that rejoice in thy light,
And bless thy sweet beauty, fair orb of the night,
As adoring they turn to thy sun-lighted brow,
Singing: Hail! Queen of heaven, how lovely art thou!

THE LAST REQUEST.

When in the grave my form shall sleep,
   Oh! plant a pensive willow near,
Whose boughs above my tomb shall weep,
   And wave their vernal tresses there;
So when the strife of man is heard
   Above the minstrel's long decay,
The tree by nature's zephyrs stirr'd,
   Shall breathe her music o'er his clay.

When in the grave my body lies,
    Oh! plant some violets o'er the sod,
Whose incense through the air may rise,
    As sweet as Love's first prayer to God;
And as recurring years shall fling
    Their virgin-smile upon my dust,
The flowers above my form shall spring,
    As sweet as Hope's immortal trust!
When in the grave my ashes rest,
    An evergreen, plant o'er my tomb,
That when the winter shrouds my breast,
    Above its snows may fadeless bloom;
Like Faith undying—over death,
    Proclaiming life by Mercy given,
And hallowing death with loving breath,
    As sweet as Christ's last prayer to heaven.*

NOTTINGHAM CASTLE.

An age the old castle a ruin hath stood,
In the place where we view it uplifted on high,
With its rock sinking down to the Leen's ancient flood,
And its walls rising upward in state to the sky;

---

* Luke xxiii. 34.

And there the great halls are exposed to the blast,
That once were the state-rooms in which did abide
The once-glowing life of the far-distant past,
In the days of its long-perished grandeur and pride;
For their glory departed at last from these halls,
And left them deserted by all but decay,
Till they shrunk to the broken and fire-shattered walls,
Whose hoary old ruins here moulder away;
No more to their bowers shall the fair dames return,
That radiant with beauty, once smiled on the scene;
No more shall they glide round these walls to discern
The pride of the pageant of years that have been;
But cold o'er their relics the centuries shall flow,
And dark o'er their ashes oblivion shall creep;
And green round this ruin the ivy shall grow,
And still in its shadow the memories shall sleep,
Of the youth and the beauty and power which no more
Shall return to the precincts where once they bare sway;
For the state of the time-conquered chieftains is o'er,
And their fair dames for ever departed away;
Yet the riflemen now for our period renew
The state of the warriors whose pageant is o'er,
Who mailed in bright armour yon postern flashed through,
Riding on the proud steeds that shall prance there no more:
And whilst round this ruin the martial strains roll,
The assembly that sounds of our warriors to-day;

A glimpse of the mailed knights may gleam on our soul,
As we gaze on our chivalry's gallant array.
And for years the old castle a ruin shall stand,
In the place were we view it uplifted on high,
With its rock sinking down to the Leen's ancient strand,
And its walls rising upward in state to the sky;
As the light of the morning upon it shall shine,
And the red clouds of evening around it shall wave,
Like the glory that shone on the chiefs of its line,
And the banners of monarchs who rest in their grave.

THE NEW ZEALAND EMIGRANTS' GREETING TO OLD ENGLAND.

Dear friends of our heart who in England abide,
How oft do you think of the days that are o'er?
When together we sate by the bright fireside,
In the far-distant land we shall visit no more;
For as o'er the wilds of New Zealand we roam,
The scenes of the past often dawn on our view,
As fondly we think of the far-distant home,
And the green fields of yore, where we wandered with you.
Yon sun that is sinking afar in our skies,
Will arise on your shore as he sets upon ours,
Illuming the fields that once gladdened our eyes,
All sparkling with dewdrops and fragrant with flowers;

Remembrance beholds them now bask in his beams,
As they smiled on our gaze in the days that are o'er,
When together we roamed by the clear-gushing streams ;
That water the land we shall visit no more.
And oft shall remembrance unto us display,
The friends and the country so dear to our heart,
While the songs of the exiles to both shall convey,
The blessing of love but with life can depart,
Which fondly now breathes o'er the world-parting main,
The greeting we send to your far-distant shore,
Awaking the utterance that answers again,
From the friends and the land we shall visit no more.
And oft o'er our spirit that utterance shall sigh,
Through the wilds of New Zealand afar as we roam,
It shall breathe on the winds as around us they fly,
The remembrance of love and the music of home ;
Which amid all the changes of swift-flowing time,
O'er the white-foaming billows betwixt us that roar,
Unchanged shall transmit to this far-distant clime,
The voice of the land we shall visit no more !

SONGS OF MERCIA.

PART SECOND.

Sacred Poems.

THE SABBATH.

Should man not give to God a day,
   Who gives him all the seven?
Shall we not that command obey,—
   A Sabbath claims for heaven?
That day of grace by Mercy blessed,
   Of earth and heaven the union,
That Labour's weary life might rest,
   And taste God's sweet communion.

Blessed day of heaven! on which the sound
   Of worship from the nations
Goes rolling upward through the round
   Of countless generations;
Oh! may our spirit e'er accord,
   With all thine high emotion,
And keep the Sabbath of our Lord,
   A day of true devotion!

Bright morn of God! amidst the night
   Of time that spreads before us;
On which through Christ first dawned the light
   Of life immortal o'er us!

As sacred as thine hallowed ray,
   From Mercy's throne descending;
Oh! may we ever keep God's day
   Through ages never-ending.

For oh! on earth 'tis heaven to rest
   From earthly care and sorrow,
And feel the beam shine on our breast
   Of God's eternal morrow;
Our souls ennobling with the ray
   That wakes our adoration,
To worship on His holy day,
   The Saviour of creation!

PSALM OF THE TEMPLE.

Around the aisles how grandly rolls
The psalm a thousand voices sing.
The worship breathing of their souls,
To heaven and earth's o'erruling King.
Sublimely pealing forth its praise,
In tones that roll above the choir,
The mighty organ o'er us plays,
Like some archangel's thunder-lyre.

Come, let our voices join with their's,
That with the past's commingled be ;
And like a flood through time now bears
Its worship to eternity.
Upon the swelling flood of song,
Which from the past its stream doth send ;
Our praises shall be borne along,
And with the future's worship blend.

For ages past this psalm they sing,
Was sung by lips no more shall sigh,
And centuries hence these words shall ring
Above the grave in which we lie.
Then let our voices blend with their's
That with all time's commingled be,
Evoking down on nature's prayers,
The answer of eternity.

PRAISE.

Come, let us sing to the Lord who created
Our being, and bless Him for life that He gave :
And worship the God from whose throne emanated,
The day-spring of glory that brightens the grave ;

Dreadful and dark would be earth's desolation,
But for the Saviour who lighted its gloom,
With the mercy that shines over life's termination,
And sheds heaven's day on the night of the tomb :
Come, let us sing to the Lord who created
Our being, and bless Him for life that He gave ;
And worship the God from whose throne emanated,
The day-spring of glory that brightens the grave.

Still through the dangers that yet may distress us,
Father of mercies ! oh ! guide us to thee ;
Still through the troubles that yet may oppress us,
Saviour of nations ! our Star of Hope be !
Still from thy might, Lord ! the strength let us borrow,
Our weakness to bear up through time's troubled day;
And guide to Thy joy through the storms of all sorrow,
That yet may arise, Lord ! to darken our way !
Come, let us sing to the Lord who created
Our being, and bless Him for life that He gave ;
And worship the God from whose throne emanated,
The day-spring of glory that brightens the grave !

GOOD AND EVIL.

Where the grace is—Father !—grace increase!
Where repentance—Father !—give it peace !

Where the faith is—Father!—bid it grow!
Where the doubt is—Father!—make it go!

Where the right is—Father!—give it power!
Where the wrong is—Father!—make it cower!
Where the love is—Father!—raise it high!
Where the hate is—Father!—bid it die!

Where the truth is—Lord!—let it be known!
Where the falsehood—God!—let it be shown!
Where the good is—Father!—bless it all!
Where the ill is—Father!—make it fall!

Where the oppressed are—Father!—set them free!
Where the oppressors—Father!—make them see!
Turn the wicked, Father!—from their ways,
With the prayer, oh Lord!—that ends in praise!

THE ANGEL OF FAITH.

I dreamt I stood within a far-off clime,
Amidst the darkness of the pagan time,
Where ancient woods a city did surround,
Within whose walls I saw a christian bound
Amidst the flames which leapt around his form
To blast his being in their burning storm;

While from the crowd around him rose a cry,
Of savage exultation to the sky,
As stood the christian martyr in the flame,
While from his pallid lips these accents came :—
"The Angel, Faith, my fainting flesh upbears,
Who through the centuries of two thousand years,
Now speaks unto the states ye ne'er shall name,
That yet shall rule the shores your Cæsars claim,
Of which the truth shall as the soul inspire,
That here ye vainly strive to quench in fire;
But past the bounds of your forgotten grave
That god-like Faith shall rise like Christ to save,
And bless the future with the truth I trust,
Above your fallen empire's scattered dust;
Thus from your cruel fire's life-torturing pain,
Now speaks the faith that over earth shall reign:
Hark! hear ye not her accents on the wind;
But, no! your ears are deaf, your eyes are blind
Unto the vision to the spirit given,
That from your flames of torture soars to heaven."
Lo! as the martyr thus addressed the crowd,
In dauntless accents ringing clear and loud,
Compelling many by his words of awe
To shrink before the vision that he saw;
His burning body yielded to the flame,
Whose jaws of fire devoured his mortal frame;

And as he down into that furnace fell,
And lifeless lay amidst earth's burning hell;
Amidst his firegrave's red and roaring light,
An angel's form methought, shone on my sight,
Of solemn aspect and celestial mien,
More tranquil than the depths of heaven's serene ;
Who from the lurid glare of that dread morn,
Thus spake unto the ages yet unborn ;
Lo ! from Jehovah's baptism of fire,
Stronger than death, Immortal Faith aspire
Above the darkness of this pagan clime,
To be the ruler of the future time :
The spirit of whose life this faith shall be,
And give their name and nature to the free,
Who never shall be bound in Cæsar's chains,
But worship God in Jesu's hallowed fanes.
Behold ! and learn why God's omniscient will
Permits the good to feel the scourge of ill,
See ! in the deepest pain that flesh can know,
Is born the highest power that earth can show,
Which o'er the fallen pagan-fanes shall soar
To worship Him the future shall adore,
Bidding the souls its virtue shall inspire,
Thus rise unconquered out of evil's fire :
Above the anguish of its flames to know
The immortal life and truth through faith which flow;

Whose strength has here the powers of hell defied,
Clasping their flames of torture like a bride;
Nerved by the Spirit's animating breath,
Behold the faith which triumphs over death,
To reign with Christ o'er future years to be,
Till nature's time sets in eternity;
When Hope and Faith their sceptres shall resign,
And all creation, Love, shall bow to thine;
As thus that angel's accents murmured there,
Like heavenly music through the troubled air,
Illumined by the dread fire's ghastly gleam,
Lo! I awoke and found it was a dream.

PATIENCE.

We do not pray, oh Father-God to Thee,
That we may never feel the stroke of ill;
But that our life e'er true to right may be,
Through every wrong—let men judge as they will.
For whilst we here upon this world abide,
We must expect to suffer grief and pain;
On stormless paths the pilgrims cannot glide,
That seek the eternal heights of truth to gain.

Yet human ignorance for thy grace must pray,
And nature's weakness for Thy help will sigh

To give us strength to tread the upward way,
And patience which shall all assault defy.
Unto our being grace and strength impart,
That we in patience may our souls possess;
And with Thy faith, rejoicing in our heart,
May bravely bear our burden of distress.

Still onward! onward! let our motto be,
Aye, upward! upward! bid our being rise,
With faith unconquered that descends from Thee,
To lead from stormy shores to cloudless skies.
Whatever wrong may then our life defame,
Or on our spirit its oppression fling;
The soul within us like a star shall flame,
And o'er the night of death immortal spring.

With beauty shining from Thy sinless sphere,
Whose brightness shall the powers of hell defy,
To eclipse the soul that shall its glory wear,
Or cast it down from God's eternal sky!
We do not pray, oh Father-God to Thee,
That we may never feel the stroke of ill;
But that our life e'er true to right may be,
Through every wrong—let men judge as they will.

PSALM OF INNOCENCE.

Inscribed to C. B. H., and E. S. H.

The inward calm that virtue knows,
Whose sunshine lights your soul to day,
The peace which innocence bestows,
Oh, ne'er let passion cast away;
Man's happy memory of the past
And happier hope of future joy,
By virtue round the soul is cast,
Which naught but sin can e'er destroy.

Fair as the landscape of the spring,
All fresh with dew and gay with flowers,
Where sweetly nature's minstrels sing,
Amid the green and fragrant bowers;
Doth life around the spirit shine,
That innocence doth now invest,
Which gives to even life's decline
The joy with which its youth was blest.

Then prize above all earthly things,
The grace which far surpasses all,

The good that round our being springs,
Which wealth or fame or joy men call ;
For know that virtue is the sense
Of all our happiness below,
And that devoid of innocence,
No happiness we e'er can know.

DOUBT.

'Tis doubt's despondency that makes us fail,
   Oh, King divine ! in loyalty to Thee ;
Inspired with faith, our spirit can prevail
   Against whatever ill our life may see.

For when we know there is a God above,
   Whose providence o'er-rules all things below,
And feel upon us fall His smile of love,
   We can o'ercome all ill that man can know.

But 'tis, oh Lord ! when we in doubt are lost,
   And in the darkness can no haven find,
Before the tempest from our anchorage tost,
   We then despair of virtue and mankind.

Then comes the strife that takes away our rest,
   And turns us often from Thy truth away,

Until Thy grace descends upon our breast,
    To change our course with truth's eternal ray.

Then may the sun as likely backward roll,
    From its meridian height to where he rose;
As to the night of doubt turn back the soul
    From that clear dawn of truth that round it flows.

Still onward like the sun its march must be,
    Higher and higher must its pinions rise,
Aspiring, Lord! from nature's night to see
    The setless noon of love's eternal skies.

No cloud of doubt our soul shall then o'ershade,
    No storm eclipse the light by mercy given,
Which, Lord! shall shine when nature's sun shall fade;
    With beam more glorious o'er Thy hateless heaven!

PSALM OF MERCY.

How fair is Thy mercy, oh! Father of light,
How sweetly it shines on calamity's night,
Transforming the teardrops of trouble, to showers
More sweet than the dewdrops that water the flowers:

More bright than the dawn of the beautiful day
That chases the darkness of nature away;
So smiles on the bosoms in sadness that pine,
To change it to gladness Thy mercy divine:
How fair is Thy mercy, oh Father of light,—
How sweetly it shines on calamity's night,
'Transforming the teardrops of trouble, to showers
More sweet than the dewdrops that water the flowers.

Let the music of gratitude breathe from our heart,
The thanks to our Father it fain would impart;
Let the psalm of our blessing ascend, Lord! to heaven,
As sweet as Thy blessing unto us is given!
How fair is Thy mercy, oh! Father of light!
How sweetly it shines on calamity's night,
'Transforming the teardrops of trouble, to showers
More sweet than the dewdrops that water the flowers!

THE ANGEL OF PEACE.

I sighed as I sank down to sleep on my pillows,
   As again through my spirit a poet's lay rung,
Which breathed o'er my being like strains o'er the billows
   Whose music from some land of glory is sung;
When a vision of Heaven arose o'er my slumbers,
   Which an angel of light to my soul did display,

Who, striking her silver harp, chanted these numbers,
    As wrapp'd in the deep trance of slumber I lay.

Sweetly I came through the clouds of thy sadness,
    Stilling the storm, with the calm made it cease,
Blessing thy down-trodden life with the gladness
    Breathed from the lips of the angel of peace;
Long had'st thou struggled and sore had'st thou striven
    With all that oppression upon thee had piled,
When, like the angel of mercy from Heaven,
    The angel of peace on thy misery smiled.

Think'st thou I came through the night of thy sorrow,
    To pour the sweet mercy of Heaven on thy breast,
But to depart from thy soul on the morrow,
    No more to return to the life I had blessed;
No! by the prayers that evoked me from heaven,
    To raise up thy trampled-down life from the dust,
Not for a moment to mock thee was given
    The peace that to Heaven exalted thy trust.

Whilst thou art true to the spirit that brought me,
    (Sent by the Father from Christ's happy sphere)
To raise up the down-trodden being that sought me
    Shall I be with thee to comfort and cheer;

Through every tempest that yet may fall on thee,
   Bright shall beam o'er thee my heaven-hallowed form
Casting the sweet spell of beauty upon thee
   Chaste as the sunbow that smiles through the storm.

Lo! when the power of injustice condemns thee,
   My greater power shall reverse its decree,
When the false spirit of this world contemns thee,
   Mine, from a better shall smile upon thee;
Bidding thee heed no unjust condemnation,
   My presence disproves and the records disclaim,
But to give thanks for my sweet consolation,
   By praying for those who God's justice defame.

Long as my ægis of light is cast round thee,
   Ne'er shall thy faith in its sure shelter cease,
Beneath whose protection no power shall confound thee;
   Or injure the spirit that's mailed by God's peace;
Man may as well try to drag God's high heaven,
   Down to the storms which beneath it arise,
As to bereave thee of grace He has given,
   Casting around thee the peace of the skies.

Pray for all creatures! and pity all scorning!
   As thou proceed'st on the pathway of right,

Lo! in reply to the sigh of the morning,
   Comes to console thee the truth of the night.
As sweetly these words through my spirit were singing
   That vision of beauty evanished away,
And I woke from my sleep as the matin-bell ringing
   Proclaimed o'er the valley the advent of day.

SUPPLICATION.

Oh! Thou eternal God, who sitt'st in light,
Above the storms of this terrestial sphere,
Yet who respondest to the earnest prayer
Of all who strive to live and act aright;
Oh! harken, Father! to my spirit's cry,
And oh, my God! unto my prayer reply,
Which in the name of Christ to Thee I speak:
Help of the helpless! Strengthener of the weak!
And through the bitter blasts that round me blow,
Oh, give me power to tread and grace to know
The path of right which leads to that bless'd shore,
To which this world's injustice cannot soar!

Oh! as upon this thorny wild I tread,
Protect, oh Lord! with Thine almighty power,
The soul that supplicates Thee, Lord! this hour,
To guard the thought of this defenceless head;

For all my arms, oh Lord! is trust in Thee,
My shield! my sword! my strength! my saviour be!
The only power that I possess is prayer,
To guard my life and light my pathway here;
I cannot even to the wrong reply,
Whose poisoned darts from souls as generous fly,
But oh! do Thou, Great God! my Guardian be!
And let whoever will—then strike at Thee!

ORISON.

O Thou! who art enthroned o'er space and time,
    Who rulest over nature's vast domain,
    As o'er his realm of light the Sun doth reign;
Oh! let our prayers unto Thy presence rise,
    As here before thy Mercy-seat we fall,
Beseeching Thee, through Christ, to hear the sighs
    Of sorrow, which for thy deliverance call!
Lord! from our souls remove all doubt and sin,
    And keep us clean and pure within,
    Oh! let us ever in Thy love believe,
    Whatever from Thy hand we may receive;
For Thine afflictions teach us good to find
Surpassing all the pleasures of mankind.

Lord! let our prayers unto thy presence climb,
   And bid eternity now answer time,
      Open Thy lips! and speak, redeeming Lord!
      That every land may hear Thy saving word.
Oh! with new life Religion's form inspire,
Give to Thy church again the tongues of fire,
To speak unto the earth like heaven's own choir,
   And to the World's remotest shore proclaim,
The goodness, power, and grandeur of Thy name;
Whose mercy shines in suns creation o'er,
Whose love embraces life, thought, space and time,
   Spreading the golden skies round every clime,
Calling mankind their Maker to adore.

Almighty Lord! beyond the dark abyss
   Of death, display the life that cannot die;
Give earth a vision of the immortal bliss,
   Whose glory shines beyond our troubled sky,
Whose utterance sometimes breathes upon us here,
   Like broken music, whispering faint and low;
Amid the discords of this stormy sphere
   The perfect harmony it cannot know.
Oh! let across the storms of nature fall
   A golden gleam of Thine eternal day,
Whose sacred light shall to its source recall,
   The World, that's wandered from Thy truth away.

And unto earth that age of heaven restore,
    When man shall curse his brother man no more.

The stormy blast, the earthquake and the fire,
    Precede thy coming, Oh! Eternal Sire,
        Who art not in their tumult—but when o'er,
            Thy still small voice shall speak to earth once more;
And man shall hear it, hearing shall obey,
The voice that bids him rise to mercy's day.
    The cloudy pillar that o'er earth doth glide,
        Into a cloud of fire shall change at last,
And to the promised future man shall guide,
    Which shall transcend the desert of the past,
E'en as the golden glory of the morn;
    Outshines the night, o'er which the day is born.

Before that day shall dawn Oh! Lord of all,
    Or ere the troubles of this time shall cease,
Oh! let thy mercy on thy sufferers fall,
    And balm their aching wounds of pain with peace;
Oh! let thy inspiration through them roll,
    Till from each bleeding heart and wounded brain
Shall gush the music of the immortal soul;
    Which was not formed for ruin but to reign,

In worlds more glorious than yon cloudy sun,
Beneath whose beam its being was begun.

With Thine eternal power
    And Thine almighty arm,
Protect our souls this hour,
    And with thy blessing calm
To peace the billows, Lord of all unrest,
Whose stormy surges roar across our breast:
Oh! stretch Thine arm of light around our sky,
    As from the sun the rays of morning stream,
And bid the glory of Thy mercy lie
    Upon the souls that pray to find its beam;
Oh! let Thy spirit on our life descend,
    And all our thoughts, and words, and works attend;
And like the covenant-angel with us go,
    Across the desert, to the promised shore,
Unto whose noon the prayers of nations flow,
    And to whose heaven the psalms of ages soar;
Wafting to Thee, above destruction's sod,
The last appealing sigh of man to God;
That Thou! who from the darkness of the past,
    Bade this existence into being flower.
Wilt from the grave of nature wake at last,
    The life imparted by almighty power;

Calling it from the night of death, to be
    Inheritor of Thine eternity *

THE INVISIBLE INFLUENCE.

There is an influence which doth flow
    On all who pray and act aright,
Whose power they both can feel and know,
    But which eludes the sense of sight;
And when they sometimes let a day
    Elapse without a living prayer,
So faint becomes that heavenly ray,
    It often seems to disappear.

But when to God their voice they raise,
    With teardrops trembling in their eye,
Then vividly upon them plays
    That guiding influence from the sky:
It falls like peace upon the heart,
    Like healing dew on nature's pain,
And doth unto the soul impart
    The wisest thoughts e'er left the brain.

---
* First published under another title, May, 1863.

With every grace and gift 'tis fraught,
    It nerves the soul with every power,
By nature's weakness vainly sought,
    Unless they from that influence flower;
Through sorrow's gloom it sheds the light
    That ne'er to pleasure's eye was given,
To misery's prayer imparts the might
    That is not earth's, but comes from heaven.

THE EXILED GODS.

Part of the angels once who peopled heaven,
Forgetting who it was that made them blessed,
Became so proud as they surveyed their state
Of heavenly beauty and unfading youth,
Celestial glory and perpetual joy,
As to misdeem that all which made them great,
Did from some good inherent in their life,
The merit dwelling in themselves proceed;
Of which, at length, they so enamoured grew,
That of it they became idolatrous,
And worshipped as the source of all their good,
Before the face of Him who gave it them.
Whereat God grew displeased to see their sin,
Insult His gentlest love with hateful pride,

And cloud with ill the heaven He formed for good;
And after bearing with them for a while,
His justice then prepared their chastisement.
The heavenly virtues and celestial powers,
Of which the angels had become so proud,
He from them took away ; and left of all
The blessings that were theirs, but naked souls,
Like discrowned monarchs, stripped of all their state,
Iu which they erst sate on the thrones of heaven.
And then unwilling to destroy them quite,
His mercy pitying the wretched souls,
Which shivered stark beneath stern judgment's blast;
He cast them in a trance, wherein they lay,
'Twixt sleep and death as sleep's 'twixt death and life,
And underneath the shadows of the past,
Out of whose darkness He had called their life,
God placed their all-unconscious life again.
Then from that shore of souls where He had placed them,
God walked into the garden of the Lord,
Which men call nature, and 'mid all its worlds,
Another formed—which with mysterious laws,
He linked with that whereon they lay entranced.
Then from the dust of that last world He'd formed,
And filled with shapes of life before unknown ;
His power almighty bade two forms arise,
To be the mansions of the immortal minds,

Whom He designed to rule the world He'd made;
Into whose frames two angel-souls were drawn,
By the occult attraction of the law,
Wherewith God joined the world material to
The world of spirits where the angels slept,
So mortal bodies, souls immortal shrined.
And for a space forgiven of God, they lived,
With some far memory of their first estate,
Lighting their souls as midnight stars the sea,
As innocent as God created them.
Until by pride again they fell from heaven,
And then were banished to sin's wilderness,
Where they in numbers grew and multiplied;
And as each new-born babe appeared on earth,
An angel-soul was breathed in it from heaven,
By the unchanging law that married mind
Unto the matter in which it was born;
Within whose life eclipsed, the angels lost
Remembrance of their former glorious states,
And only knew themselves as sinful men.
Though, still a sense of something more divine
Than all the dying beauty of the world,
In which the exiles dwelt in banishment,
Lingered within their spirit's fallen shrine;
As some faint influence of their childhood's days
Awakes within the breast of guilty men,

Striving to lead them to its innocence,
So, with the angels in their fallen state,
A sense of something happier spake within them,
Seeking to lead them back from banishment.
Whence comes it that on earth is often heard,
Faint echoes of the strains once sung in heaven,
Sighed by the exiles in their banishment;
Which as men hear, awake within their souls
Strange longings after some unknown estate
Of never-dying truth, and love, and joy,
Whose speech forgotten breathes along their souls,
A sense of something higher than the world
And happier than the life which on it dies;
And then as mortal tears bedim their eyes,
Immortal prayers ascend through them to heaven,
Asking of God the answer which He gives,
Unto the souls, to whom at last there comes
An intuition of their first estate,
Informing them that they are exiles here,
Abiding in a land that's not their home.
While strange mysterious longings through them thrill,
For which they have no language, for the clime
They have forgotten, but aspire to know
In prayers that move the pity of the skies,
As they behold the exiles weeping for
The innocence on earth they lost in heaven.

Then God in mercy sends the angel, death,
To lead the exiles back again to heaven,
Where Mercy decks them in their former state,
And sets them on the thrones of bliss in heaven,
From which they fell, and places on their brows
The starry crowns of love, pride cast away,
While all the choirs of heaven breathe forth such strains
Of joy, that heaven would weep if it had tears,
Beneath the rapture of the immortal songs,
That welcome back the lost from banishment.

PSALM OF EXPERIENCE.

Oh! Thou who kindest art unto the soul,
When to the sense, Thou harshest Lord! dost seem;
Oh! through our ignorance let thy graces roll,
To guide us to the heaven from which they stream.
Oh! let us not, great God! ourselves deceive,
Or with presumptuous mind our souls betray,
But give us grace in Jesu to believe,
And faith to climb up on His hardest way.

That perfect way designed to train the soul,
And to develope its heroic powers,

And give it faith to find the deathless goal,
Whose base above the crest of nature towers.
Oh! give us patience, Lord! oh! give us power,
To bear rejoicing every pang of pain,
May wring our bosom through life's troubled hour,
As here we strive Thy heaven of good to gain!

Unto our being, Lord! the grace impart,
That it may sing to Thee a life of praise,
Which, Lord! with each pulsation of our heart,
Shall bless the giver of our mortal days.
Oh! with Thy thoughts, oh! Lord! our soul inspire,
More lovely than the opening flowers of spring;
Oh! teach our souls the good their prayers desire,
That we Thy mercy to mankind may sing.

Who Thy eternal truth to man hast given,
And reared the standard of our good so high,
That it from earth directs as high as heaven,
The life that lower aimed, in dust would die.
Oh! Thou who kindest art unto the soul.
When unto sense, Thou harshest Lord! dost seem;
Oh! let Thy graces through our blindness roll,
To light us to the heaven from which they stream!

SINCERITY.

Father of Man! let thy blessing be given,
   Unto the soul of sincerity here;
Bright as Thy day-beam of mercy o'er heaven,
   Smile on that soul from eternity's sphere;
     Though clouds of wrong surround,
      Let not their gloom confound,
The life whose pulsations beat true, Lord, to Thine!
     Through the illusions,
      Of man's confusions,
Oh! let the truth of that spirit, Lord, shine!

Send from Thy heaven a bright emanation,
   Which shall with wisdom Thy children indue,
To know by the light of its pure revelation,
   The hearts that are false from the hearts that are true:
     When o'er the last, Lord,
      Darkness is cast, Lord,
Purer and tenderer bid them, Lord, grow!
     Till as they brighten,
      Bid from them lighten,
The truth which is Thine, and no darkness can know.

THE ANGEL OF DEATH.

As alone o'er the couch of the dying I hung,
When the mantle of midnight o'er nature was flung,

A fear-breathing presence suspended my breath
With awe, 'twas the grave-shrouded phantom of death,
Whose form by the low couch arrested stood there,
As this anthem was breathed through the star-lighted air.

Hark over earth, how the music of heaven,
Sings of the life which to man shall be given :
Rise up! oh! pilgrim of earth from the night,
Rise up! oh! spirit redeemed to the light,
To be blest in the morning of heaven with the breath
Of life, as you rise from the darkness of death.

Brightly upon you shall mercy's sun shine,
Fadeless above you its bowers shall entwine,
Deathless around you the love-flowers shall blow,
Grandly before you the broad streams shall flow;
Softly the glory shall fall on your breast,
Sweetly the blessing upon you shall rest !

Come from the gloom that now darkens earth's sod !
Come from its graves to the gardens of God !
Come from its sorrows! come from its sighs !
Come from its pain to the peace of the skies !
Where the vallies of heaven around you shall ring
With the welcome the angels immortal shall sing !

As over the dying this love-breathing hymn,
Was breathed from the shore of the bright seraphim,
The form of mortality yielded its breath
To the stroke of the grave-shrouded phantom of death,
As its soul on the wings that by Mercy were given,
Arose through the night to the morning of heaven!

DESPONDENCY.

I am aweary of the storms of time,
   And fain, oh Lord! unto that world would fly,
To which no cloud of trouble e'er shall climb,
   To dim the light of God's eternal sky.

Prepare me, Lord! to meet the stroke of death,
   And purify my soul that it may rise,
When this weak mortal form resigns its breath,
   Unto the peace of love's unclouded skies.

Oh! hear the utterance of the life Thou gave,
   And bid it, Lord! from death aspire to see
Thine arm-almighty stretched across the grave,
   To lift its life to mercy and to Thee.

Oh! leave me not unto myself alone,
   But with Thy heavenly help my soul sustain,

Oh, bless me, Father! from thy glorious throne,
  And give me grace that I may heaven attain.

Oh! leave me not on this tempestuous wild,
  Where bitter blasts unceasing on me blow;
But lead me where Thy love has ever smiled,
  Where I the blessing of Thy peace may know.

Oh! raise me from a world to justice blind,
  Where I the justice of the just may see;
Oh! save me from the mercy of mankind,
  And show the mercy of a God to me!

Where kinder than affection's teardrops fall
  Upon the lifeless features of the dead;
The light of heavenly love descends on all
  The souls who on the shore of mercy tread.

And when my body sleeps within the grave,
  Oh let the truth to which I bent my knee,
And to whose good my life its worship gave,
  Attest, oh Lord! the truth that dwelt in me.

When death shall cast its night around my frame,
  Bid through its darkness shoot a heavenly ray,
Which like the cherubs' turning sword of flame, [clay.
  Shall guard from this world's wrong my breathless

KEEP THY HEART WITH ALL DILIGENCE; FOR OUT OF IT ARE THE ISSUES OF LIFE.

  Can spirits false to good believe,
  The truth that is as true as heaven?
  Can souls impure the rays receive,
  Which by the holiest light is given?

  Can chaos with creation blend?
  Discord with harmony combine?
  Disorder to the height ascend,
  Round which the laws of order shine?

  Alas! the fault is in our heart,
  When from the truth we turn away,
  Which cannot to the false impart
  The light of truth's eternal day.

For true must be the mortal breast,
On which the Holiest sheds the beam,
By which the immortal soul is blest,
With good past all that ill can dream.

ST. PETER'S DREAM.

Upon the evening of the Sabbath-day,
St. Peter up a mountain went to pray,
He'd seen his master breathe his latest sigh,
And crucified with malefactors die ;
And to the sepulchre his form consigned,
Wherein seemed lost the Saviour of mankind,
And worn out with the tumult of the week,
St. Peter sighed the prayers he could not speak ;
By dismal doubts and doleful thoughts oppressed,
He laid at last his weary form to rest ;
Where deepest slumber o'er his senses stole,
And where this vision passed before his soul :
He dreamt, he stood upon Mount Olive's crest,
And saw Jerusalem beneath him rest,
With its majestic shrine and massive walls,
And Herod's mighty tower and stately halls ;
And as he gazed upon the glorious sight,
So weirdly gleaming through the solemn night,

In all the grandeur of unbroken pride,
Behold! the Tempter stood by Peter's side,
And as with terror he stood rooted there,
His mocking voice thus hissed in Peter's ear:
"Lo! where he lies, in yonder rock-sealed grave,
From which no prayer shall waft, no God shall save,
Nor fond disciples steal away his form
From those who guard it for corruption's worm,
As I in pity come this hour to thee,
To show thy soul what shall hereafter be;
Look yonder!" As he spake, St. Peter gazed
Upon the city, which before him blazed,
As though th' abysmal fires had broke their bound
And with volcanic force burst from the ground,
In sudden conflagration fierce and fell,
Wrapping Jerusalem in the fires of hell,
Amidst whose rolling smoke and raging flame,
The roar of battle and destruction came,
Big with the utterance of ten thousand cries
Of vengeance and despair that rent the skies.
While shuddering with horror, dread and awe
Around—within the temple—Peter saw
The Roman legions moving—slaughtering all
The Jews, who there despairing fight and fall;
As sinks Jehovah's temple in the fire,
Wherein His name and nation both expire.

"See!" Satan said, as Peter shrunk aghast,
While that dread vision thus before him past,
" See ! of Jerusalem the end decreed,
Beneath whose fall shall perish Abraham's seed,
Thus trampled down at last by Gentile hordes,
His sons shall perish by the Roman-swords,
And in Jerusalem's ruin find the grave,
From which the Hope of Israel shall not save;
Thus shall His name depart from Jacob's shrine,
And all the kingdoms of the earth be mine,
Thus shall Jehovah's glory hence be hurled.
And Israel's name be blotted from the world ;
And can'st thou still, fond fool, thy Christ adore,
Who breathless rests upon the skyless shore ?
Behold Him in the tomb, in which he lies,
And bid Him from yon sepulchre arise :
Snatch from corruption's grasp his breathless clay
And bid unyielding death resign his prey,
Or here to me, poor fool, resign thy trust,
Weak as thy thought, and worthless as His dust."
" Avaunt ! false Spirit ! hence !" St Peter cried,
" Bright as the daybeams that o'er darkness glide,
Firm as the hills, unshaken as the skies,
My faith thy falsehood, king of hell, defies,
And by my soul His promise is believed,
Who never His disciples yet deceived,

That from the tomb, wherein His body lies,
Christ, who rais'd Lazarus, shall Himself arise."
Lo! as he spake, the fire dissolved away,
And in uninjured state Jerusalem lay,
Fair as a city dawning on the sight,
Through all the scatter'd vapours of the night,
Lit by the first ray of the golden morn,
Whose smile proclaims another day is born.
And as they gazed, an earthquake shook the ground,
The mountains quaked, the rocks were rent around,
As rising, like the sun, from nature's gloom,
Jesus appeared, ascending from the tomb;
Robed in a blaze of uncreated light,
To which the day of earth appeared a night,
And from whose sinless and eternal ray
The Tempter like a phantom shrunk away,
While Peter knelt His Master's form before,
And lost in wonder, only could adore.
As Jesus smiling stood before his sight,
As fair as God arrayed in Mercy's light,
And thus addressed him: " Peter! thou shalt see
Past Satan's ill, My good that yet shall be,
Look hence! and see beyond this age and clime
The truth unwritten of the future time:
See! from the flames where God appears to die,
The daybeam shine of His eternity,

Untrampled down by Rome's imperial hordes,
Triumphant lightning o'er their broken swords,
To strike the gods they worship to the dust,
And o'er them throne the Christ who is thy trust,
Who stronger than their armies shall arise,
Above the grave in which their empire dies.
Look round the earth and gaze on all its climes,
Beneath the far-off days of future times;
Behold the unborn millions who shall live
The life of Christ, who died that life to give;
To save men from the error of their way,
And souls redeem from ill, who'd gone astray;
To be my chosen sons, my spiritual seed,
The worshippers of God in thought and deed;
How could I see them lost in error's night,
And groping blindly there for Mercy's light,
Nor long upon their life to pour the ray,
For which men pined, but knew not how to pray?
Behold them stand round every clime and age,
The countless children of Christ's heritage;
Gaze on the sumless souls My death shall save,
For whom I came to fill a martyr's grave;
Look down along the length'ning course of time,
Stretching away through every age and clime;
Age after age behold my gospel glide,
Advancing o'er the earth like ocean's tide;

From wrong converting nations to the right,
And turning men from darkness to the light;
The life of millions raising up from sin,
Unto the life in Christ their souls shall win;
Bright type of resurrection yet to be,
From Adam's death to My eternity;
Oh! not in vain have I salvation brought,
Not vainly has Christ suffered, loved and taught!
Not vainly on the cross has Jesus died,
For from the cross shall God's redemption ride,
Conquering and to conquer through all time,
In every city and in every clime,
And light the gloom, by error round them cast,
And by my good retrieve men's evil past:
Lo! from the fire that seemed to be the grave
Of all the truth, which God to man e'er gave,
Stronger than time or death it shall aspire,
Out of the flames of Israel's funeral pyre.
And riding o'er the earth shall conquering go,
As strong as God to conquer all below;
O'er nation after nation it shall run,
Far as the beams of heaven's unclouded sun,
Till earth's long darkness shall depart away,
And on mankind shall shine redemption's day,
Till all false gods shall from the earth be hurl'd,
And Christ shall reign upon a brighter world;

'Thousand of ages hence thy soul shall see,
The truth from heaven, a dream now shows to thee,
When all thy trials, Peter! shall be past,
And thou shalt rest with Christ, thy Lord, at last."

Here from his soul the vision passed away,
And Peter woke beneath the dawning day,
And to the sepulchre he ran to see
Christ risen from death to God's eternity.†

MARCH OF LIFE.

Through all the darts that round us fly,
  Oh God, who sit'st above!
Oh, lead us to Thy hateless sky,
  Of perfect peace and love.

Oh, guide us through the storms of time,
  To where no storm shall roar;
Oh, lead us to Thy starry clime,
  On heaven's unclouded shore.

Through all the dangers of our way,
  Through all the snares of ill:

---
† First published about September, 1862.

Oh God! our only Hope and Stay,
    Do Thou protect us still.

'Mid earth's injustice dark and dread,
    Oh Lord! our faith sustain,
And give us grace the path to tread,
    That shall Thy truth attain.

Our all of hope is fixed on Thee,
    We hope in man no more;
Oh, let us Thy salvation see,
    When this life's storms are o'er!

AFFLICTION.

Increase, oh Lord! our trust in Thee,
    And take affliction's gloom away;
Oh, let us, Father! live to see
    The good return, for which we pray.
Accept, oh! Lord! our earnest prayer,
    Which in His name our lips repeat,
Who on the cross our sins did bear,
    And answer from Thy mercy-seat.

Yet, if we must endure this pain,
   Oh! give us strength to meet its blow,
And patience, Lord! that shall sustain
   With praise, all pangs that we must know.
Oh! let our faith but stronger grow
   Beneath the stroke of every ill,
That from our hearts to heaven may flow
   Obedience to our Father's will.

MAN'S CHAOS.

Let thy grace through nations gushing,
Lord! like dawn through darkness flushing,
Lord! like day round nature rushing;
   Sweep away the wrong for ever!

Wherewith nations gall each other,
Wherewith masses justice smother,
Wherewith brother blesses brother,
   In the world by man created.

Care! the heart of love is blighting,
Fear! the head of life is whit'ing,
War! the peace of heaven is smiting,
   In the world by man created.

Hark! what means this fearful sighing?
Hark! what means that fearful crying?
Misery living!—misery dying!
    In the world by man created.

Oh! what nerves with trouble aching,
Oh! what hearts with anguish breaking!
Oh! what minds in madness shaking!
    In the world by man created.

Pity! weep o'er desolation!
Mercy! dawn on every nation!
Father, rise! and bless creation,
    With the world which thou created!

Through kings and peoples send a shivering
Through nature's troubled heart a quivering,
A shock-almighty!—heaven-delivering,
    From the hell by man created!

Flood all souls with grand emotions,
High as heaven and deep as oceans,
Race away all narrow notions,
    From a world regenerated.

PSALM OF THE SOUL.

Oh! Thou unseen, yet all-beholding God,
Who sit'st beyond where nature's suns can climb,
Yet hearest every prayer,—from earth's low sod
That's breath'd to Thee amid the storms of time;
Oh! hearken, Father! to my earnest prayer,
Which in the name of Christ I breathe to Thee,
The Martyr-Son, who came from heaven's high sphere
The great Redeemer of mankind to be.
And from Thy Mercy-Seat, oh God! incline,
And on my weakness now the strength bestow,
That shall not, Lord! to evil e'er resign,
The trust in life and death Thy truth to know;
My strength alone is weakness, that must fall,
And unto evil all its good resign,
Whose power shall brave the worst assault of all,
If armed, All-father! with the grace of Thine.
The ice of winter's warmer than the breath,
That blows across the sordid world of man,
Which hourly blasts the innocent with death,
And on misfortune places guilt's dark ban;
But Thou art kinder than the prayers of love,
More pitiful than all the frozen tears,
That e'er were wept by human hearts above
The graves of death, throughout life's passing years,

Thy thoughts the thoughts of all Thy worlds transcend,
In thy unbounded love our love doth lie,
But like the clouds their shadows o'er us send,
Above which towers the sun-enthroning sky!
Yet, though Thou art exalted past our thought,
Thou did'st not form the least beneath Thy care,
Which watches over all with mercy fraught,
That ever answers to the voice of prayer.
Thine eye all-seeing, now my life surveys,
 As night with all its stars beholds a sea,
That tranquil grows beneath the calming gaze,
That looks o'er time from heaven's eternity:
Oh! let my prayer unto Thy presence rise,
And bid Thy blessing on my spirit fall,
More sweet than dew distilling from the skies,
To quench the thirst and bless the life of all.
Around my being bid the accents flow,
Fraught with the praise of that exalted sphere,
Whence sing the blest to all that pray below,
Who suffer now as once they suffered here.
Oh! breathe into my life the peace and joy,
Which form the air of love's celestial day;
And like its Spring breathe over earth's annoy,
To charm the winter of this world away.
Oh! let Thy grace and strength upon me flow,
To heavenly peace that turn all earthly pain,

And give to man by e'en destruction's blow,
The immortal life that over death shall reign.
Oh! let Thy blessing now upon me fall,
In answer, Lord, unto my broken prayer,
And bid thy mercy, Father, shine on all,
Who suffer wrong upon this stormy sphere.
Have pity, Lord! on all who pray and weep,
Oh! stab earth's icy heart with truth divine;
Bid Mercy's breath unfreeze the polar deep,
And o'er its breast Thy heaven unclouded shine
The day of earth is darkened with the woe,
Whose groans ascend from all her pagan shores,
Hark! how from earth to heaven a cry doth go,
Which God's deliverance now for man implores.
Humanity is sick of all the war
And weary of the woful peace of man,
And to the God of mercy groans afar
By His great advent to remove the ban.
Oh! come to save mankind as erst Thou came,
To bless the world, created, Lord by Thee,
Not as on Sinai's top, enrobed in flame,
But clad in mercy, earth from sin to free.
Descend from heaven, to overcome man's ill,
Again o'er chaos, Holy Spirit, move,
Shoot through earth's savage heart a far-off thrill,
A sense divine of Thine almighty love!

Oh! breathe humanity into the breast,
Which ne'er before a touch of pity knew,
And with the fruits of love let lands be blest,
Where but before the thorns of hatred grew.
Oh! smite the rock with Thine almighty power,
Till from its breast again a river flow,
Where every thirsty heart may drink this hour,
That prays the fountain of Thy love to know.
Bestow, oh! Lord! on every lonely heart
The affection now for which they vainly pine,
Again heaven's manna to the earth impart
And change man's desert to a land divine !
Unto the future give a fairer fate,
Than ever gave to man the awful past,
Convert earth's pagan to a christian state,
Which as Christ's kingdom shall for ever last.
Bid Mercy stretch her angel-arms from heaven,
To bless the world with good for which we pine,
Sweet as the morning unto Eden given,
Before man sinned against Thy love divine.
Make all men christians called, christians indeed,
With heavenly charity inspire their breast,
Convert the worldling from his barren creed,
And give the storm-worn heart of sorrow rest !
Take from the haughty white the baseless pride,
Which looks upon the much-wronged black with scorn,

Oh! bid Thy wisdom, Greatest! o'er them glide,
Which treats not so the least of woman born.
On human hearts misjudged beyond all thought,
And wronged beyond what mortal tongue can tell,
Oh! send Thy mercy down with pity fraught,
Whose power would turn to tears the flames of hell!
Breathe through their life the spirit all-divine,
Whose virtue's stronger than all human power,
And in the darkest night doth brightest shine,
To rapture turning e'en destruction's hour.
Awake repentance in each erring heart,
To guide them out of sin's tremendous gloom,
And grace and blessing to their souls impart,
Till fair as childhood's flowers their being bloom.
Bid justice be the law of all the earth,
Let not a mortal spurn another's fall,
But strive to raise them to that second birth,
The Lord of life would fain impart to all.
Pour forth Thy Spirit, Lord! on every shore,
As through the breaking storm the sun doth shine,
In vain of man redemption men implore,
It only can proceed, oh! Christ, from Thine!
Oh! shine around the earth, eternal sun!
Pour forth Thy Spirit in a quickening flood,
In vain to man for help in need we run,
Which only can be given by Thy good.

Oh! let thy glory shine on every shore,
To give the light to earth that heaven first gave!
And bid religion's self to man restore
The speech of life that sings beyond the grave!
Come, like a rushing wind, Celestial Dove,
With all thy tongues of fire on earth descend,
Whose burning inspiration shall remove
The ills with which we vainly now contend.
Bid judgment's mockery crucify no more
The souls whereon Thine image is impressed,
Nor ignorance cast confusion nature o'er,
To blast with ill the life that God hath blest.
Scatter mere human judgments to the wind,
But one is right that e'er on man was given,
That men are all to truth and justice blind,
Unless when lighted by the grace of heaven.
Oh! let no ghoul sit on the minstrel's grave,
But bid the angel, Love, above it weep,
Such tears as those he vainly shed to save
The heart he loved from death's unwaking sleep.
Yet take not one oppression from his mind,
Or from his past a single pang remove.
They were allowed by heaven that he might find
Beyond destruction's grave God's deathless love.
The path of anguish once in tears he trod,
The springless desert, where his youth was cast,

His spirit taught to know the truth of God,
Which led him to the cross of Christ at last.
In His name, Lord! accept this broken prayer,
And let my psalm of life now answered be
By good, that every suffering soul shall share,
That pray to find it as they kneel to Thee!*

MORNING HYMN.

Oh! let Thy mercy on us shine,
As bright as morning's golden ray,
And with its glory, Lord divine!
Oh, chase our every doubt away.

Oh! let Thy grace upon us fall,
As soft as heaven's refreshing showers,
Whose drops the fruits of Autumn call
Out of the wreck of summer's flowers.

THE MANSIONS OF ETERNAL REST.

Ye mansions of eternal rest,
 Around the fields of heaven, which shine

---

*First published under another title in the first month of the present year, 1863

More glorious than o'er nature's breast,
    Appears the orient's crystalline :
We pray beyond this world forlorn,
    Your palaces of light to see,
Which fairer than the gates of morn,
    Ascend above eternity,

From this o'ercast terrestial frame,
    We fain unto the world would fly ;
Whose palaces of crystal flame,
    Arise above our stormy sky :
And over nature grandly gleam,
    Whose systems darkly round them roll,
Whose ages towards the temples stream,
    Designed for man's immortal soul.

We long upon the world to gaze,
    To which the prayers of time aspire;
Whose mansions o'er its darkness blaze,
    Like cities built of silver fire.
With fields of glory spread around,
    More beauteous than the skies of morn ;
With all the constellations crowned,
    Whose stars the dome of night adorn.

Beyond corruption's starless grave,
   Oh! Mercy! give us wings to soar,
Which o'er the night of death shall wave,
   And waft us from destruction's shore.
Unto a world of light and love,
   Unto Thy heaven of peace and joy;
Whose life immortal smiles above,
   The storms that nature's peace destroy.

There resting in unfading bowers,
   Immortal love to Christ shall raise;
Above its never-dying flowers,
   The psalm of never-ending praise.
To Him the life who has restored,
   Which death shall never more destroy;
And through that life immortal poured
   The music of eternal joy.

"THE GOOD LORD PARDON EVERY ONE."

2 Chron. xxx. 18.

" The good Lord pardon every one,"
   Whose soul has gone astray,
Yet fain again would walk upon
   Religion's happy way.

"The good Lord pardon every one"
  Who would from sin depart,
And seek the grace denied to none
  Who seeks with contrite heart.

"The good Lord pardon every one,"
  For we all sinners be,
And hope of grace is given to none,
  Except, oh! Christ, through Thee!

PSALM OF JUDGMENT.

Oh! Thou to whom the psalms of nations soar,
  To whom the prayers of all the ages fly;
As move their myriads over nature's shore,
  Unto the grave in which they all must lie!
Before Thy Mercy-Seat, O Lord! we bow,
  And in the name of Christ invoke of Thee,
That Thou wilt hear the prayer we utter now,
  And let Thy blessing, Lord! our answer be;
Oh! with Thy Spirit, Lord! our souls inspire,
  And by Thy power, O God! our life defend;
And let the wisdom that our souls desire,
  Our thoughts, our actions, and our life attend.

Protect, oh Lord! the souls that cast away,
    Their trust in all defence but Thine alone :
More strong than all the armies that to-day,
    Are round the confines of the nations thrown;
Amidst the troubles of this stormy time,
    Against oppression, Lord! our rights sustain,
And guide our footsteps to Thy deathless clime,
    Which seek on earth its sinless shores to gain.
Oh! let Thy mercy, Lord! our life surround,
    And light the darkness of this turbid air;
With beam so bright that nothing shall confound,
    The souls on which its blessing shall appear.
We do not ask to be exempt from woe,
    We only pray whate'er our portion be,
That Thou wilt give us grace Thy good to know
    And faith to give our hearts to truth and Thee ;
The glory of the sun may turn to gloom,
    And darkness cover all the eternal sky,
Destruction quench the stars that space illume,
    And bid the life of all creation die :
But, oh! no power can quell the deathless soul,
    On which the mercy of its Maker shines,
Imparting power that man cannot control,
    To dim the glory of Thy great designs.
When judgment's thunder-storm shall shake the world,
    And all the systems of yon starry sky, .

Shalt melt amidst the fires around them hurled,
    And in the lightnings of Thy glory die;
The souls that to Thy truth their worship gave,
    Secure amid the wreck of worlds shall be,
And rise immortal over nature's grave,
    Through judgment's fires, to mercy and to Thee!

PSALM OF PEACE.

Oh! lead us, Lord, into Thy sighless air,
Exalt our being to Thy stormless day,
On which no cloud of trouble shall appear
To take the pleasure of our life away;
But where the deathless flowers of love shall bloom,
And where the thornless bowers of bliss shall twine
Beneath the morn, whose light shall heaven illume
With beams more blest than on the earth can shine,
Where after life's long storm the souls shall rest,
Whose hearts on earth to God their worship gave,
And in the fadeless gardens of the blest
Shall taste the peace that smiles beyond the grave,
Where deep and tranquil as a mighty stream
Their thoughts shall through their minds immortal flow,
And sweet as flowers unclose to nature's beam,
The love shall blossom which they there shall know;

Where softer than the dews of heaven distill
Their grateful blessing on the vernal sod
Shall flow around their souls, the breath shall fill
Their life immortal with the grace of God!
Where fairer than the day of nature rolls
Its golden glories o'er the blooming plain;
The mercy shall descend around their souls,
That gives to them the loved and lost again!
Oh! lead us, Lord into Thy sighless air,
Exalt our being to Thy cloudless day;
On which no shade of sorrow shall appear,
To take the pleasure of our life away.

IN REMEMBRANCE OF E. K. II.

Lament not, oh! mother bereaved, for the child,
Whom the angel of death from thy bosom hath ta'en,
When so lovely it bloomed, and so sweetly it smiled
In the home, which its beauty shall bless not again.

More kind than the tear-drops that fall from thee now,
O'er the place, where so lovely in death she reclines
With her fair little form and her innocent brow;
The smile of God's love on her spirit now shines.

Untainted by sin and untroubled by woe,
She has gone to the world, where no shadow can be,—
To a region of light that no evil can know,
To abide with the blest, who no sorrow can see.

And who to the troubles of time would recall
The dear little babe, who has past from their gloom,
To the light of the morning, which shines beyond all
The darkness that rests on the land of the tomb.

She blossomed below like a fair little flower
Of affection, to us that its beauty displayed, [hour.
And was borne from the world, where it bloomed for an
To the world where the flowers of love cannot fade.

And, oh! its remembrance shall hallow our heart,
And the sweetness it breathed shall attract to the shore
Of the love, which that flower to our life did impart,
Of the love, which that flower to our life shall resto¨

So, blessing Thee, Lord! for the gift Thou bestow
We bless Thee, oh! Lord! for the gem Thou hast
Whose spirit from heaven now points out the road
We must travel on earth, to embrace it again!

PSALM OF HEAVEN.

Oh! say what is heaven?—a beautiful clime!
A region untouched by the troubles of time,
Where the vows of our love and the prayers of our youth
Shall return to our age with the freshness of youth.
And the hopes of our innocence turned into joy,
No storm shall o'ershadow, no time shall destroy,
In that heaven of delight, in that region of rest,
Where love shall again clasp the lost to its breast;
And affection refined from the mists of the clay,
More loving and lovely shall grow in the day,
Where reason shall rise o'er the shadows of time,
To the wisdom revealed in its heavenly clime,
Where the powers of our nature expanded shall be,
And the wings of the soul shall at last be set free,
That once like a bird in its dungeon confined,
Vainly beat at the barriers, which prisoned mankind,
Whose boundaries shall shut in the spirit no more,
That far past their confines sublimely shall soar,
With free thought and fresh force and new feelings fired,
And powers unknown to its first state inspired,
Whose pinions shall wave o'er a heaven of delight,
As the wings of the eagle rejoice in their flight,
As it rides on the blast of the free-blowing wind,
Looking down from God's heaven on the grave of mankind

As the soul shall look down from the heaven of its rest,
On the world where it died ere it lived with the blessed!

ODE.

Oh Thou Eternal and Almighty King,
   Enthroned beyond the gaze of nature's eye;
Before whose face the choirs of mercy sing,
   As round Thy throne the worlds of glory fly;
Oh! let my psalm, All-father! answered be,
   Which in the name of Christ I breathe to Thee!
And give me grace, O Lord! that e'er shall guide
   My steps aright, what e'er my soul betide;
Though wrong with obloquy my life defame,
   And slay me for what man's oppression wrought,
And mutilate my memory with the same
   Injustice, which eclipsed my life and thought;
Yet, God of truth! whate'er my portion be,
   Oh! guide me right through every wrong to Thee!

Lord! guide my soul!—then let all wrong that can
   Fall on this feeblest head like mountains piled,
To overwhelm me with oppression's ban,
   And crush my life out on destruction's wild;

Though chains of mountains were upon me cast,
  My truth through all their bars would burst at last;
Though matter's worlds were heaped upon my dust,
  Through nature's walls would burst my deathless
    trust
Like quenchless flame no force can downward bend,
  But which unto its fountain will aspire,
And through the rocks of nature upward tend,
  To reach the source from which first came the fire,
Unquenchable as light that Jesu sees,
  Flashing o'er time from two eternities!

Though this poor name be to oblivion flung,
  And all the record of my thought forgot,
Though no remembrance of my life remain,
  To blossom like a flower upon the spot,
On which I suffered, and on which I sung,
  The music that breathed peace upon my pain;
The heavenly harmonies whence it did roll
  Around my being, shall sublimely play,
When this life's discords shall have passed away;
  And breathe eternal worship through my soul.
And all the clouds, my brain once darkened here,
  And all the storms that on my being frowned,
Shall vanish in the day-beam of the sphere,
  Whose life with e'er increasing good is crowned!

Beneath whose setless day my spirit shall survey
    The truth to which my reason here was blind ;
And see before me shine in words of love divine,
    The end of all the sufferings of mankind ;
Teaching why virtue's gain was here a loss,   [cross !
    And why God's throne on earth—the Martyr's

No matter then, if wrong my life pourtrays,
    As what I was not ; if Thy truth records
Me, what I was ; and to Thine eye displays
    The thoughts too sacred to be touched by words :
Thy justice, Lord ! shall balm my every wound,
    And through my trance of suffering breathe the
Of peace eternal from the painless shores,   [sound
    Where love the fountain of its life adores.
Let judgment's mockery, treat me as it will,
    Thy peace within me shall defy its power,
And stand unwounded round my being till
    This mortal life to life immortal flower,
Beneath the beam to which to night would fade,
    The light of all the suns round earth arrayed.

Yet not for this poor self alone, I pray,
    Thou God of love ! I pray for all mankind !

Oh! bid them cast the wrongs of time away,
  And with a Christ-exalted heart and mind,
A nobler future for the children find
  Than was the unnatural age their fathers knew,
Upon whose life such blasts of evil blew.
  Oh! bid them to the heights of love aspire,
Which rise o'er hate's low scene like alps of snow,
  O'er whose white thrones of grandeur gleams the fire
That like God's smile doth light the world below,
  Calling men from the depths of earth's despair,
The light of God's eternal joy to share!

Lord! bid the nations to Thy peace arise,
  Beneath the attraction of Thy gentlest power,
Which man created, not to be the prey,
  For ever of the ills he is this hour;
But that through nature's pain his prayers might rise
  To evoke the wisdom of love's long delay,
And turn the nations from their thorny way
  Unto the paths where beauty's roses flower,
And on whose fields the dews of blessing shower,
  That in fresh life the wasted world array;
Oh, bid the nations, Lord! to Thee return,
  Chanting the psalm of peace unto the sound

Of music, that like Mercy's tears shall yearn
    To voice the thoughts for which no speech is found,
Amidst the adoring praise, the nations yet shall raise
    Unto the King who is with mercy crowned,
As o'er earth's myriad isles the spring of beauty smiles,
    Whose vernal fragrance floating o'er the ground,
Blending with strains that roll along the sod,
    Shall rise to heaven as man returns to God!

Return to Thee! Thou light of every beam
    Of wisdom which now shines upon the soul:
Return to Thee! O Source of every stream
    Of happiness, that over time can roll:
Sun of affection! Sovereign of the whole
    Creation, which Thy laws of love control:
Soul of all Beauty! who doth all out-shine,
    Exalt man to the heights of love divine!
And thus, All-Father! answer all the prayers
    Whose sighs, to thee, oh Lord! have uttered been,
In the deep language of th' unspoken tears
    Of souls who through their falling showers have seen
A beauty gleam—and heard a music glide
    Sweeter than all the worship man e'er sighed!

Why should our spirit ever then complain
    Of grief and suffering?—oh, let those repine,

Whose life untouched by trouble doth remain,
   On whom the rays of pleasure ever shine ;
E'er basking in whose beams we must resign
   The light that comes from darkness to incline
Our souls unto the wisdom of the skies,
   Whose oracles o'er reason darkly rise ;
Yet from the grief of this unhappy time,
   Lord ! teach my spirit to evoke a strain,
Fraught with the echoes of Thy heavenly clime,
   Whose grace with Mercy's peace balms nature's pain,
Breathing the inspiration of the state,
   Passing our love, as that transcends our hate !

Oh, by this life's long sorrow, teach my soul
   To evoke a harmony from all this woe,
These awful wars, and life-eclipsing peace ;
   Which long as nature's tears through time shall flow,
O'er nature's suffering shall like music roll   [cease ;
   From that blest shore where suffering's pain shall
Teaching men to o'ercome ill with the might
   Of Him, who died the sacrifice of wrong ;
And out of pain and weakness was made strong
   To conquer man, time, sin and death, with light.
For me, though after death the power of wrong
   Transform my living truth into a lie ;

The might of mercy that inspired my song,
   Shall breathe its music through my latest sigh ;
As sinking to my grave I pray to God to save
   The future from the oppressions of the past, [pride,
And by his grace, men guide from wrong and hate and
   Unto the truth and peace and love of Christ at last,
And all His children guide from wrong and hate and pride
   Into the truth and peace and love of Christ at last !*

THE CHILDHOOD OF HEAVEN.

Oh ! why are we not to the spirit all true,
That made childhood so blessed and its beauty so fair ?
As it spread round our being as fresh as the dew,
Which sparkling arose through its heaven-lighted air ;
Oh ! why from its peace do we wander away,
To discover at last, as we sigh for its rest,
That the heaven-hallowed beam of its innocent day,
Illumines no longer our care-darkened breast !

Yet, let us return to the childhood again,   [found,
Whose peace was more sweet than all pleasures we've
Since we left it behind us to seek but in vain,
For aught like the charm of its joy-haunted ground ;

---

* First published, May, 1863.

For the beauty of love, and the blessing of peace,
And the glory of good to the spirit are given,
Which the joy will impart that again shall not cease,
And our manhood transform to the childhood of heaven!

VICE AND VIRTUE.

Oh, what a blessing virtue gives,
And what a curse doth vice bestow,
Upon the life in vice that lives,
Unto the life no vice doth know;
For peace and joy in good inhere
And strife and storm in evil dwell,
In paradise that virtue sphere,
And from it cast all vice to hell.

Then let us walk on virtue's way,
Which leads to higher virtue still,
Nor be by evil led astray,
That sinks us down to deeper ill;
So high the path of good doth rise,
So deep the track of ill doth go,—
The first will lead beyond the skies,
The last conduct to cureless woe.

PSALM OF CONFIRMATION.

What argument can turn our spirit back
From that good way it is so sweet to tread,
Or draw our steps aside into the track,
O'er which confusion's darkness now is spread.

No! we must still pursue that happy way,
On which we find such heavenly joy and peace,
That we again from them can never stray
Into the desert, where their life would cease.

But on with strength'ning faith our life shall go,
And never from that happy way depart,
On which we find such good upon us flow,
As clears our reason and expands our heart.

Oh! yes! we will that heavenly grace obey,
Which through the night of anguish on us shone,
To guide our life to truth's eternal day,
And light our being up to Mercy's throne.

For by instruction that cannot deceive,
We've learned to know the way of truth at last,

In whose eternal good we must believe,
Confirmed by deep experience of the past.

And so rejoicing onward day by day,
We bless Thee! Lord! who such a way hast given,
As that on which we for Thy blessing pray,
While walking on the path of peace to heaven.

Let those this way of happiness deride,
Who never on the path of pleasure trod,
Where little children innocently glide,
Nearer than Wisdom to the life of God!

PSALM OF HUMANITY.

Lord! let Thy mercy on the nations flow,
As round the world the quickening sunbeams fly,
To make its latent life to beauty blow,
Beneath the blessing of the bounteous sky.

For, oh! the desert of man's life doth pine
To feel the light of Thy retrieving day,
Across the long eclipse of evil shine,
To chase the shadow of its night away.

Unseal the latent fountains of Thy love,
That frozen lie upon this wintry shore,
And bid the waters o'er the desert move,
Which Eden's verdure shall to earth restore.

Oh! with the heavenly grace man's soul inspire,
That soft as pity's sighs o'er earth shall fall,
And sweet as music breathed from Mercy's lyre
The care-worn nations shall to God recall.

On man's obdurate heart, oh Father! shine
Like nature's summer on the polar snow,
Until its life shall feel Thy touch divine,
And soft as pity's tears beneath Thee flow.

For 'tis the hardness of the human heart,
That covers o'er the earth with strife and wrong,
Then, Lord! to man the grace of heaven impart,
And make it gentle as affection's song.

Unclose the eyes that now to truth are blind,
Upon each stony heart Thy Spirit pour,
Oh! bid mankind have mercy on mankind,
And blast each other's life with wrong no more.

But let the love of man to God reply,
As echo answers now the psalm we sing,
And o'er the abyss of the vaulted sky
Waft nature's worship up to Mercy's King!

WORSHIP.

We worship Thee, oh! glorious God!
    Who governs't all below;
Whose goodness bade around nature's sod
    Its flowers of beauty blow.
Its pleasures to the earth who gave
    Their peace unto the skies,
And bade out of destruction's grave,
    Immortal life arise.

We worship Thee, oh! glorious God!
    Who reigns't o'er all above;
And yet as low as this low sod,
    Doth manifest Thy love:
Which is unbounded as the power,
    From which the treasures flow,
Which give unto our life this hour,
    Whatever good we know.

We worship Thee, oh! glorious God!
    Whose love Thy works proclaim;
From flowers that garland nature's sod,
    To suns round heaven that flame;
Whose constellations o'er the skies,
    Thy glorious power display;
Who bade them out of darkness rise,
    To turn it into day.

We worship Thee, oh! glorious God!
    Who pities't misery's prayer,
Who turns't away affliction's rod,
    And gives't to man's despair,
Hopes fair as flow'rets of the lea,
    Which blossom here so bright,
And answers't man's appeal to Thee,
    With love more sweet than light.

THE ADVENT OF PEACE.

As on my couch in slumber I reclined,
Behold! this vision pass'd before my mind:—
Methought I saw a plain beneath me lie,
Above whose green breast spread the boundless sky,
O'er which a great black thunder-cloud was spread,
Dark as the pall, which mantles o'er the dead,

Within whose threat'ning shadow nations stood,
Praying, methought, for some invisible good;
And as I gazed appaled upon the cloud,
That over nature stretched its heavy shroud,
Lo! through its centre burst an angel-form,
Bright as the sun, that laughs away the storm,
Beneath whose smile like mists which melt in air,
That black cloud brake and seemed to disappear,
Revealing as its rack away was borne,
The vast expanse of heaven alight with morn,
O'er which that angel's silver chariot flew,
Just like a white cloud gliding o'er the blue,
Till in mid-heaven its snow-white steeds did rest,
As thus the angel 'Peace' mankind addressed:—
"When shall the heathen flag of war be furled,
And Peace descend from heaven to bless the world?
Weary of all the pagan-darkened past,
And praying for a christian age at last;
To cast the errors of man's youth away,
And march at last to Wisdom's heavenly day;
Which on the night of nations yet shall dawn,
And light their gloom with heaven's forespoken morn
Beneath whose beam the soul of man shall flower
To finer stature and to nobler power;
Within whose noon-day glory yet shall shine
The life and love which spring alone from mine;

That through the years of unborn times shall sing,
The undreamt joys of love's unpictured spring;
Before whose smile the wars of earth shall cease,
And God's fair world at last be blest with peace."
As rolled these music-accents round the skies,
While Peace sate throned in heaven before our eyes,
Lo! from the nations' multitudinous throng
Arose from earth to heaven this answering song:
" Hail! lovely Peace, upon our world descend,
And round our life those angel-arms extend,
To every soul that heavenly form display,
And roll the long despair of earth away,
Oh! come from heaven, sweet Peace! a world to free,
A weary world, that prays to heaven for thee;
Thy silver sceptre wave round every shore,
And bid man blast his brother's life no more,
But bless with peace a world designed for joy,
And what God formed, Oh! let not man destroy,
But from thy presence, Peace! let war be hurled,
As thou descend'st from heaven to bless the world!"
As on my ear arose that thunder-song,
From that uncounted multitudinous throng,
The vision from my spirit pass'd away,
And I awoke to greet the dawning day.

REASON AND REVELATION.

We think and toil and strive and scheme and plan,
With anxious spirit and with busy mind ;
Amid the mazes of the world of man,
The path of pleasure and of peace to find.
But think and toil and strive and scheme in vain,
With toiling reason and with troubled heart ;
The human oracle within the brain,
The clue that we invoke cannot impart.
'Till in despair we raise our eyes to heaven,
Beseeching from it those enlightening rays,
That by its mercy can alone be given,
To guide us right through life's bewildering maze.
And through the darkness on our souls they fall,
Lighting the gloom whose shadows seemed to rise
Before our gaze like death's cimmerian wall,
Impenetrable to our reason's eyes :
Cleaving the gloom as with a sword of light
Athwart whose void we deemed no ray could shine,
Opening the portals of the starless night
With glory, lightning from a power divine.
Revealing to our gaze that happy way,
So fruitlessly to find our reason strove
And brightening like the dawn to perfect day
As on that Christ-enlighted path we move.

Oh, from that pathway may we ne'er depart,
But on it see the dawn to day increase,
That comes to light our erring human heart
Through nature's night to God's eternal peace.
That path on earth of happiness and love,
Was by the Maker of this world designed;
The path of man unto the life above,
Who on no other path that life shall find.

THE WORD AND THE WITNESS.

What doth attest the word of life as true?
The Spirit, which the word of God inspired,
Without whose teaching no man ever knew,
Or understood the truth that he desired.
Without the Spirit's witness none can see
The latent truth which in the letter lies;
The light must flow upon our souls ere we
Can read what's hidden from the sense's eyes.
The height we can attain by prayer alone,
On which God's Spirit meets the soul of man,
To make the way of truth to reason known
And to instruct us in His deepest plan.
Prayer purifies the soul from pride and sin,
And as a child its innocence doth guide;
It leads us to the point that none can win,
Who is not chastened first and purified.

The point at which the still small voice of God,
In mercy's accents speaks unto the soul,
The path of life disclosing, Jesus trod,
Of which eternal glory is the goal.
Yet oft doth human frailty interpose,
And cast a cloud of passion and of sin,
Betwixt the point from which the Witness flows,
And soul immortal darkly shrined within.
For only on a mind from passion freed,
And through an atmosphere of sinless rest,
The witness of the Spirit can proceed,
Which doth to man the truth of God attest.
So from behind the vail of old there shone,
The beam on Israel which God's truth displayed,
Attesting by the light of Mercy's Throne,
The revelations by Jehovah made.
And men by reason only, vainly try
To read and comprehend their Maker's plan;
The truth to thought alone, makes no reply,
Which gives God's answer to the prayers of man.
Yet in its clearest light, when soul intent,
With eye reverted on the point would gaze,
From which the attesting light is darkly sent,
We see no sun who yet perceive the rays.
That vivify our life with heavenly light,
Beneath whose beams our fairest fancies flower;

Our deepest, highest thoughts of truth and right,
Our grandest acts of grace and deeds of power.
Upon the soul of man the Witness streams,
More glorious than the demonstrative ray
Which from the throne of star-eyed Science gleams.
Across our reason like the dawning day.

THANKSGIVING.

Oh! Thou Eternal King! whose patient heaven
Around the space and time of earth extends,
Whose mercy like the morn to earth is given,
Which on us like the smile of God descends:
We bless Thee! oh Thou Hope of man in need,
Who helpest all the children of the dust,
Whose life invokes by thought and word and deed,
The strong defence of Him in whom they trust.

We bless Thee for the day that on us beams,
Investing nature with the colors fair,
Which flow round earth in ever-changing streams,
From that far heaven where they more bright appear.
We bless Thee for the night that on us falls,
Beyond whose dome of darkness we survey
The grand star-lighted heaven that man enthralls,
As with a gleam of God's eternal day.

We bless Thee for the mind bestowed on man,
Whose mighty powers the thoughts of God enshrine,
Sublime as are the heavens which Thou did'st plan,
And beauteous as the worlds that round them shine.
We bless Thee for the affections Thou hast given,
Whence flows the happiness that blesses here,
Whose music rises now from earth to heaven,
To waft our worship to its happier sphere.

We bless Thee for the afflictions that we know,
Which come to chasten and teach us the way,
Unto the peace the world cannot bestow,
Unto the joy it cannot take away.
We bless Thee for Thy Word, on whose great scroll
Thy truth, oh! Lord! in golden letters gleams
Through nature's darkness on the suffering soul,
More glorious than the day round earth that streams.

We bless Thee for the spirit, Lord! of prayer,
That to our life Thy goodness did impart,
Which to the Mercy-Seat of God doth bear,
The ennobling worship of the human heart.
We bless Thee for the spirit, Lord! of praise,
Which sings its adoration unto Thee,
Who blessest us with all our happy days,
And with the hope of happier days to be.

We bless Thee for the Lamb's redeeming blood,
Through which man's purified from error's stain,
And through whose virtue he attains the good,
Which makes him innocent as Christ again.
We bless Thee for the goodness, from which flows
Thy answer, Lord! to every earnest prayer,
Which all the graces and the gifts bestows
That deck with heavenly flowers this earthly sphere.

We bless Thee for the grace Thou dost impart,
Which doth the assault of every ill defy,
To take away the peace that calms the heart,
That with Thy Word attunes, oh! Lord! Most High!
We bless Thee, for the truth on us doth shine,
On which no storm can ever cast a shade,
To dim the glory of the power divine,
Before whose light all storms like shadows fade.

We bless Thee for the still small voice that rolls
Its heavenly utterance over life's annoy,
And stirs the hidden fountains of our souls,
To tears more sweet than every earthly joy.
We bless Thee for the thoughts Thou dost inspire,
And words of light that to our prayers reply,

Pure as the glory of that heavenly fire,
Which speaks the wonders of the starry sky!

We bless Thee for the life by us possessed,
For all the love that to our life is given,
For all the good wherewith that life is blest,
And for the faith which points its hope to heaven:
Upon whose sorrowless and sinless shore,
We trust to bless the Christ who died to save
The life, which shall the God of love adore,
In never-ending songs beyond the grave.

THE MOTHER'S LAMENT.

(Written in Remembrance of John Lawrence, who died, October 9th, 1863, Aged 23 Years.)

In the pride of his manhood and strength of his youth,
The son whom I cherished was borne to the grave ;
And left me bereaved of the goodness and truth,
Whose life to my soul their affection once gave.
The joy of my heart and the hope of my years,
Lie quenched in the tomb where his relics recline
In the long sleep of death which regards not the tears
That gush from the depths of such sorrow as mine !

His spirit was generous and open and free,
His heart was a shrine where the truth ever smiled :
He was kind to all creatures—the kindest to me,
Who live to lament o'er the loss of my child.
And, oh ! it seems hard to this grief-stricken breast,
That the home which his spirit once lighted with joy,
Shall never again by the presence be blessed,
Of my noble and loving and beautiful boy !

Yet Faith comes—through the darkness of nature to raise
My vision afar to the love-lighted skies,
Where again on the child of my heart I shall gaze,
And the tears of my grief shall be wiped from my eyes ;

And, oh ! as they fall on the place of his rest,
I long to depart to that region of joy,
Where the son of my soul I shall clasp to my breast,
And nevermore part from my beautiful boy !

THE RIFLEMAN'S DIRGE.

(In Memory of John Hebb Newton, who accidentally transfixed himself with his own bayonet, at a Review of the R. H. R., on Bulwell Forest, and died of the injury, Friday, October 9th, 1863, and was afterwards buried with military honours in the Church Cemetery, Mansfield Road, Nottingham, in the presence of a great concourse of spectators.)

Bear him away to the bed,
From which he shall never arise,
Until the grave yields up the dead,
Whose dust in its darkness now lies ;
When the thunders of judgment shall shake
The world, and the dead shall awake
From the long sleep of death and the night of the tomb,
To the blessing of bliss or the banning of doom !

Sound his last march as ye bear him away
To the tomb, in whose bosom his fathers recline ;
Peal forth his dirge as ye carry his clay
To the mansion of darkness his form shall enshrine,
Where ages on ages like billows shall sweep,
But arouse not the dead from his visionless sleep !

Maidens around him shall blossom and fade,
Manhood above him increase and decline,
As season o'er season is round him displayed,
And century on century above him shall shine;
Cities around him shall flourish and fall,
Empires above him shall rise and decay,
But break not the slumber oblivious of all
The scenes which the future of man shall display;
All things shall change that are under the skies,
But the blue hills alone in the distance that rise,
Which unchanged shall appear as they shine o'er the scene,
The landmarks of nature to tell what has been;
While the rifleman rests in the slumber of death,
Which no change shall awaken—no beauty shall know,
More cold than the blast of the life-killing breath
Of Winter—when wrapped in his white shroud of snow,
He sinks down to rest in the midst of the proud,
In his winding-sheet dressed like a corse in its shroud.

Others shall roam o'er the scenes where he strayed,
Strangers shall dwell in the home of his youth,
Childhood shall sport where his infancy played,
And inspired the first memories of nature and truth;
Fair through the future the river shall flow,
As through the past he beheld its waves go;

Brightly the sun o'er its waters shall rise,
Whitely the moon shall ascend o'er its stream,
Lightly above it shall spring the blue skies,
Nightly upon it the bright stars shall gleam;
And all that he once beheld glassed in its wave,
Shall be glassed there again while he sleeps in his grave,
Where silence shall mantle his form in her shroud,
And darkness envelope his bones in her pall,
Protecting his dust from the strife of the crowd
Whose tumult around him unheeded shall fall,
As the swift-flowing current of time bears away
To the gulf of the past all the ages to be,
And changes the forms of the world we survey,
To the fashion of that world the future shall see,
When the temples whose newly-raised towers round us shine,
Grown hoary with age into ruins decline.

Over his ashes affection shall weep,
That would to its bosom his being restore,
Which shall never arise from his sorrowless sleep,
His form that shall chain to oblivion's shore,
Till the mountains of nature shall sink in decay,
And the heavens that shine round the earth pass away,
As night fades away in the light of the morn,
In whose glory the beauty of nature is born:

When the sound of the trumpet shall thrill through the
    dust,
And awaken the dead to the life of the just,
Whose cities of glory shall burst on their eyes,
More bright than the morn's golden clouds through our
    skies,
On the world of God's love, o'er the heaven of His rest,
Which for ever shall give to the souls of the blest;
The beauty surpassing all men can conceive,
The grandeur transcending all earth can behold,
The happiness passing all sense can believe,
Whose joy shall the spirit immortal enfold,
As the glory around it the star doth invest,
That is set like a gem in the gold of the west.

Breathe the death-prayers as we stand round the sod,
Beneath which our brother now sinks to his grave,
Let the voice of our worship ascend to the God,
Whose mercy alone from destruction can save;
Let the death-sigh of nature arise o'er the tomb,
To the Christ who alone can its darkness illume,
With hope and with blest immortality's ray,
Which enlightens man's grave with the dawn of the day
That shines beyond darkness, destruction, and sorrow,
On a world to which evil can never arise,

To eclipse with its shadow the light of the morrow
That smiles on the blest from their winterless skies,
Where Christ sits enthroned in the glory arrayed,
That was His before nature's foundations were laid!

More fair than the sunshine that lights his last bed,
Sublimely His mercy to man shall be given,
When glorious as God, He shall smile on the dead,
And welcome the just to the morning of heaven,
Which their spirits shall bless in the regions above,
That never by sorrow or sin shall be trod,
But where they shall live in the light of His love,
As far above ours as man's beneath God,
And the Saviour of sinners adore with their lays,
" Exalted o'er all human blessing and praise!"

www.ingramcontent.com/pod-product-compliance
Lightning Source LLC
Chambersburg PA
CBHW020904230426
43666CB00008B/1310